SHORT LEASH

SHORT LEASH

A Memoir of Dog Walking

and Deliverance

Janice Gary

Michigan State University Press

East Lansing

♾ The paper used in this publication meets the minimum requirements of ANSI/NISO
Z39.48-1992 (R 1997) (Permanence of Paper).

 Michigan State University Press
East Lansing, Michigan 48823-5245

Printed and bound in the United States of America.
19 18 17 16 15 14 13 1 2 3 4 5 6 7 8 9 10

LIBRARY OF CONGRESS CATALOGING-IN-PUBLICATION DATA

Gary, Janice.
  Short leash : a memoir of dog walking and deliverance / Janice Gary.
    pages cm
    ISBN 978-1-60917-359-3 (ebook)—ISBN 978-1-61186-072-6 (pbk. : alk. paper) 1.
Gary, Janice. 2. Authors, American—21st century—Biography. 3. Dogs—Biography. 4.
Life change events. 5. Human-animal relationships. 6. Dog walking. 7. Self-realization in
women. I. Title.

  PS3607.A78298S56 2013
  814'.6—dc23
  [B]   2012047839

Book design by Scribe Inc. (www.scribenet.com).
Cover design and artwork by David Drummond, Salamander Design, www.salamanderhill.
com. All rights reserved.

"Random Acts" first appeared in *The Potomac Review* 51 (Spring 2012).

g green Michigan State University Press is a member of the Green Press Initiative and
press is committed to developing and encouraging ecologically responsible publishing
INITIATIVE
practices. For more information about the Green Press Initiative and the use of recycled
paper in book publishing, please visit www.greenpressinitiative.org.

Visit Michigan State University Press at www.msupress.org

You who do not remember
passage from the other world
I tell you I could speak again: whatever
returns from oblivion returns
to find a voice

—LOUISE GLÜCK

SHORT LEASH

OCTOBER 1991

SAVANNAH, GEORGIA

Forty-five pounds of muscle and fur pulled me down a dark road with no sidewalks, no lights, and barely any shoulder to speak of. The dog was a stray I had found three days before—a smelly, exuberant hulk of a pup who had captured my heart the moment I saw him. I paused for a moment and reeled the cord in just enough to keep us in the beam of my husband's flashlight. The dog stopped straining and walked by my side. "Good boy, Barney," I said, even though I was pretty sure he had no idea that "Barney" was his name.

We walked into the night, past the ranch-style houses, past the sewer ditch filled with singing frogs, around the bend where the road curved and the shoulder widened. Once again, the dog pulled ahead, testing the limits of the retractable leash. I pressed the button to stop the cord from reeling out, but just as my thumb hit the lever, the coiling unit fell out of my hands and bounced against the pavement. The reel began spinning wildly, gobbling the cord faster and faster until it reached Barney's heels, startling him so much that, after a sharp yelp of surprise, he took off like a rocket. I ran after him, but he ran faster, terrified of the plastic monster clattering behind him like a string of Chinese firecrackers.

I could hear Curt laughing behind us. "It's not funny," I shouted back at him. Maybe it would be if I wasn't so terrified of the dog getting hit by a car.

Finally, I got close enough to step on the bouncing unit. As soon as I scooped it up, the line began unwinding again. I grabbed the cord and pulled back hard, reeling Barney in like a big fish. For the rest of the night I kept the leash locked in tight, afraid of what would happen if I let it go.

You cannot reason with a dog. I wish I could have told him that the faster you run, the louder it gets; that it's nothing, really—only a square of plastic containing a cord—but you can't explain such things to a scared animal. Or a scared person. Nothing is more terrifying than the ringing steps of an invisible pursuer.

How loud is a ghost? Let me tell you. As loud as a firecracker. As loud as tin cans tied to a dog's tail. Louder than a scream. As loud as time and memory can make it.

CHAPTER 1

OCTOBER 2001

THE ENGINE IS OFF. THE SEATBELT UNBUCKLED. THE WINDOWS ALL rolled up. There's nothing left to do except get out of the car. But I don't. Instead, I sit there, staring out the windshield at the woods beyond the parking lot, my right hand squeezed into a fist around fourteen keys, a string of beads spelling "S.O.B.," a solid brass circle, and a Big Boy juggling a hamburger in his chubby plastic hand.

Most of these keys are so old I can hardly remember what they unlock—an office at a job I no longer have, a house in a city I don't live in anymore. It doesn't matter. What matters is the weight, the heft of the brass and steel, the fact that this key ring once was taken from my hands in the basement of a church by a self-defense instructor and held up for all the women in the room to see. "Take a look," she said. "Now *this* is an example of an excellent weapon."

It's also a liability. My purse is ungodly heavy. Most of my coat pockets have holes in them. The ignition tumbler on my car has had to be replaced. Twice. "You need to lighten this thing up," the mechanic told me.

Not gonna happen.

Outside, leaves tumble across a browning meadow. Trees bow and bend in the breeze. In the backseat, a ninety-five pound dog paces back and forth, his tail thumping against the cloth seatbacks in a kind of canine Morse code: *Wow! Oh wow! The park! I can't believe we're here.*

I can't believe it either. I've been avoiding the place for years.

Walking a dog in a park should be simple. But for me and Barney, there's nothing simple about it. We're handicapped, the two of us, in ways that are invisible. To see us walking down the road, you would never guess that the smiling black Lab at the end of the leash is a fur-covered time bomb or that the athletic-looking woman behind him is incapable of walking without a four-legged crutch. There would be no way of knowing that if a dog comes too close to Barney, he turns into a killing machine. Or that if I find myself in an isolated area or an empty street late at night, my mind enters a war zone where the enemies are everywhere and nowhere.

Barney sticks his head between the bucket seats and gently nudges my shoulder. "Alright alright," I say. "I get the message."

He's the reason I'm here, after all.

I stash the keys and a canister of Mace in my pocket and reach back to hook the leash onto Barney's collar. As soon as the door opens, he leaps onto the tarmac, pulling the retractable cord out to its full length so he can anoint a small bush at the edge of the lot. We set off in the direction of the picnic tables, following the tree line abutting the meadow. While he runs as far as the leash will let him, I move slowly, straining to catch any sound that will indicate the presence of a person or a dog. Birdcalls float through the air. Leaves scuttle across the ground. We're alone. At least I think so. No one else around except for me and my dog-shaped shadow.

With Barney leading the way, we walk a few yards and then a few yards more, and before I know it we're almost to the picnic area. My steps are lighter, my breathing easier, when, suddenly, I hear the sound of shuffling leaves coming from the direction of the woods. Panic shoots through every nerve ending. I reach for the Mace in my coat pocket. As my fingers wrap around the canister, a squirrel darts out of the woods.

For a moment, all I can do is stand there, shock mixing with disbelief. *Jesus,* I'm thinking. *Spooked by a squirrel.* The animal stops several yards away and watches Barney and me as he nervously gnaws on an acorn. His eyes keep flitting back and forth, and it's obvious what's on his mind: *Am I safe? Should I stay? Or should I run?* I study his face, noting the flat eyes set wide apart so he can watch for predators on either side.

"No need to worry," I say to him. His eyes dart to the left. To the right. He's not buying it. And I don't blame him.

We turn toward the meadow, leaving the squirrel to his foraging. While Barney stops to sniff the leaves of a small holly, I take a deep breath and look around, amazed at how beautiful this place is, even on a gray day. My heart is still beating from the squirrel panic, but I hear the breeze moving through the treetops, *shoosh, shoosh,* like a mother calming a baby. My breathing slows down. I slow down.

A few minutes later, I'm about to pull the keys out of my pocket to head back to the car when I'm stopped by the slow-motion dance of a leaf in the wind. Even though the sky is cloudy, even though the leaves are yellowed and dull and beginning to curl at the edges, there is a profound beauty to this place. As I stand there, I hear branches dropping, squirrels running. And something else, something I haven't heard for a long time: the sound of silence in my head.

For a moment, I drink in the quiet like water, like a woman who has been thirsty for ages. The wind washes over the leaves—a great wave signaling something coming. Not a bad thing. Not a good thing. Just change.

I usually don't welcome fall in Maryland. In fact, I dread it. As the light wanes, the dark begins pressing in against me. Sometimes it takes over.

This time though, it's different. The leaves aren't falling, they're twirling and gliding, diving off branches like acrobats without a net. The sky is cloudy but alive, filled with birds moving in practiced groups among the treetops. Squirrels chide each other to get moving. The park is readying itself for a season of quiet. It feels like I'm being readied, too, though for what I'm not sure.

As we make our way toward the parking lot, Barney pulls ahead (an alpha habit I have tolerated, even encouraged, over the years), steering us back to the edge of the woods. When we approach the tree line, I pull him back. He looks at the woods, then at me, his eyes pleading, telegraphing the words he cannot say: *There's important information here; we must go on.* He's trying so hard to be understood that I can't refuse him. Despite my doubts about moving away from the meadow, I let his leash out and follow along. While he stops and sniffs a fringe of sticker bushes, my eyes wander into the woods. The wine-like scent of fermenting leaves and earth overwhelms my senses, and before I know it, I'm reeling like a drunken sailor on the decks to another time, another forest, and the roads and towns beyond it where there were no leashes, no collars, and no limits to where I would go.

When I was a girl, I dreamed away whole afternoons in the woods, setting up household in trees, listening to the symphonies of streams, making pretend castles out of termite-infested stumps. I looked into the soft brown eyes of deer before they ran, saw fox slink into bushes, watched snakes slither across sun-warmed rocks. When the sound of guns popped in the distance, I was scared only for the deer, never for myself. Nearby, acres of apple and pear orchards bloomed in the spring, and when fall came I picked as much as I could eat, stepping around the bees that swarmed in great numbers over rotted fruit on the ground. Later, I climbed out of bedroom windows to walk under the stars, rode around town in hippie vans, traveled out west with two pairs of jeans and $70.00 in my pocket. I camped under velvet skies in the desert, crashed in seedy apartments in strange cities, bummed cigarettes, bummed money, bummed rides with questionable men, and rode off with only the clothes on my back and some weed in my pocket. I was wildly, willingly, stupidly free.

And now, look at me. Afraid to walk in a park with my dog.

I'm a woman on a very short leash.

CHAPTER 2

FALL 2001

BARNEY AND I RETURN TO THE PARK THE NEXT DAY AND THE DAY
after that. And we keep coming back until three weeks of walks have piled
up behind us. One morning, as we drive into the park, I see a new banner
on the entrance gazebo announcing the upcoming Halloween Barkin' Bash.
It's a dog party, complete with costume contests, prize giveaways, and free
treats, but it's a party we can't attend. I make a mental note to stay far away
from the park next Saturday.

When we get out of the car, the air smells of apples and earth. As usual, I
head toward the picnic area, but Barney reels his leash out in the opposite direction, hot on the trail of a good, fresh scent. Since there's no one else around, I
figure what the heck—why not let him go where he wants? Nose to the
ground, he sniffs his way across the field to a concrete drainage ditch at the side
of the road, no doubt tracking some critter who has made his home in the pipe.
While Barney sticks his head in the culvert, my eyes wander to the forest across
the road where the trees sway back and forth in unison like a line of dancers.

Several minutes go by as Barney investigates the sewer pipe. The movement of the trees is hypnotic; it's as if they're beckoning to me with their

twiggy fingers. I step into the road toward the woods. Then I take a few more steps. Barney, done with his inspection, walks right past me, his leash unspooling enough for him to cross over to the other side. Without even thinking about it, I follow. And just like that, our walking grounds have expanded.

Standing on the grassy strip between the road and the forest, I'm rather stunned at what has just happened. Before now, I've been careful not to venture beyond the small patch of meadow just beyond the park entrance. Day after day, it's been the same routine: pulling into the same parking lot, parking in the same parking space, walking in the same picnic area. Now that I'm across the street, I see things I've never seen before: a long slope of woods, the outline of a picnic pavilion in the distance, mountain laurels sparkling in the sun.

The road is six feet wide at best, but for the past three weeks it might as well have been the Grand Canyon. It's startling to realize how boxed in I've become, relying—insisting, actually—on the worn patterns of my habits to move me through the days. There's nothing wrong with indulging in the same routines every day: drinking your favorite tea at the same time or having the same breakfast every morning. But I'm well aware that some of my routines go beyond preference or habit, often entering another realm altogether, like when I have to fold my clothes just so *or else;* or when I can't go back inside my house once the door is locked *or else.* If I don't obey these ridiculous commands, something bad will happen. Or something good won't.

There is a desperate, obsessive quality to these thoughts. I know it, but that doesn't mean I can let them go. Sometimes, I'm held captive by my own thoughts for days, weeks, until I fight back and refuse to obey the whispering warnings in my head. Coming to the park for the first time was one of those acts of defiance. And coming back the next day was another.

Barney stops to examine a pine branch while the woods unspool before me. As I stare into space, my mind wanders back to when I thought nothing of leaping across continents, much less a road—any road, anywhere. I was a girl running as far as possible from her past. A girl who believed that such a thing was even possible.

In the spring of 1972, my freshman year at Ohio University had just ended. Out of forty-five credits taken that year, thirty had a grade of "PR," which meant pending requirements, which meant I spent more time smoking pot, writing songs, and hanging out in the southern Ohio countryside than in class. Not that I cared. I wanted to be a musician—a singer, a rock star. It seems foolish now—not exactly the best career move for a young woman—but then it felt like the right thing to do, the first step of a trajectory I had been planning my whole life. I moved back home for the summer and tried to keep up my hippie lifestyle, smoking pot in the bathroom with the fan on and listening to Procol Harum and Rolling Stones records for hours on end. At night, after my mother had passed out on the downstairs couch and my sister and brother were asleep, I'd slip out the window of my second floor bedroom and hitch rides into town. When a friend invited me to join her on a short trip out west to California, I joined her, bringing only the money in my pocket and the clothes on my back. When I got back, I returned to Athens and Ohio University, but only to live with friends and to make up a year's worth of incompletes.

The following summer, I found myself living at home again. My mother bought me an old Ford Galaxie, which I drove back and forth from the Cincinnati suburbs to Clifton, home of the University of Cincinnati and the town's resident hippie population. I spent long, lazy afternoons there, hanging out with musicians and periodically crashing in their roach-infested apartments. I briefly considered returning to Athens. Then, I came up with a better plan. I would move to California, find a band, and climb my way to the stars. All I needed was a little start-up cash.

When September came around, instead of registering for classes, I took a job waitressing at a Perkins Pancake House off I-71 outside Cincinnati. For five long months, from midnight until 6 A.M., I served platters of eggs and waffles to truckers, drunks, and insomniacs until enough money was saved to put the plan in motion. By February, I was ready. There was only one thing left to do.

Locking my bedroom door from the prying eyes of my mother and younger siblings, I cleared off the top of the nightstand next to my canopy bed and placed a candle, three brass coins, and the *I Ching/Book of Changes* on it. Rubbing the coins between my palms, I silently repeated a single question before flinging the brass disks onto the table where they skittered across the painted surface before settling to rest, two face-side up and one blank-side up: young yang.

I had discovered the coins in a small shop in San Francisco's Chinatown the summer before. According to the sages, the responses from the *Book of Changes* were of such import that they could save one from a lifetime of folly. I wanted to believe that was true, but consulting the pages of the *I Ching* was more an act of willfulness than of faith—a desperate attempt to influence forces beyond my control, the same forces that had already buffeted me around like a kite in a March sky.

Four years earlier, my father had died. His death was a sudden and shocking event that set in motion a series of events that I could never have predicted. We moved from New Jersey to Ohio to be near my aunt. My mother, who had never handled the family finances, was suddenly flush with cash from my father's life insurance. She bought a new house, a new car, a new everything. Loosened from my father's tight grip and supported by my mother's loose purse, I set out to make a new life of my own. Out went the Villager clothes and polite good girl manners. In came the ripped jeans, ironed hair, and hippie lifestyle. It was as if all the fences had been taken down around me and I was a wild horse, not concerned or even cognizant of the dangers of running off into the world unbridled. But as much as I tried to divert myself from the truth, it was there, lying just beneath the surface of my *fuck-you* persona: I was flying blind. And I knew it.

I threw the coins five more times, marking a solid line for yang and an open line for yin in my journal, until there were six lines stacked up over one another, representing one of the 64 hexagrams of the *I Ching*. The question I asked was this: *Should I move to California?* The answer was Hexagram 36: Ming I/Darkening of the Light. Injury.

Not exactly what I was hoping for.

The image aligned with Hexagram 36 was that of the sun sinking below the earth. The sequence read: *Expansion will certainly encounter resistance and injury. Hence there follows the hexagram of Darkening of the Light. Darkening means damage, injury.*

I could feel my heart sinking like the sun in the hexagram. It didn't sound like a good omen. But maybe I hadn't read it right. Like most *I Ching* revelations, the pithy commentary in the hexagram contradicted itself with each line, foretelling of disaster in one but perseverance in the next. I combed the lines—one representing King Wen, another Prince Chi, all battling for control and confusing the hell out of me. No matter how I interpreted it, though, most of the lines foretold of disaster. It was a mistake. It had to be. The truth was, I had already made my decision. All I wanted was for the *I Ching* to back me up.

I repeated the question and threw the coins again. This time, I got Hexagram Number 4: Meng/Youthful Folly.

> *The young fool seeks me.*
> *At the first oracle I inform him.*
> *If he asks two or three times, it is importunity.*
> *If he importunes, I give him no information.*
> *Perseverance follows.*

For a moment I sat there stunned, as if someone had just slapped me across the face. How could a stupid book and stupid fake ching coins know that this was my second try? I looked around the room half expecting to see someone floating in the air above me. I read on. The first line spoke of humiliation, as did another one four lines down. But the fifth line said *childlike folly brings good fortune.* And the second line stated *to know how to take women brings good fortune.* I didn't know about the taking women part, but the line mentioned fortune, so it couldn't be all bad.

Perseverance followed. Three days after the *I Ching* reading, I stashed some clothes, a bag of pot, and $240 saved from waitressing into my bag and headed out to California. The fact that I had nowhere to stay or any kind of job prospect didn't faze me in the least. I had the names of friends of friends and that was good enough. At sunrise, I met my ride near the university and jumped into a rundown van filled with long-haired guys I barely knew. In Louisville, the van merged onto I-64 and headed west. For the next two thousand miles, I followed the sun to where it sank into the earth. Three months later, I returned, a different girl altogether.

CHAPTER 3

NOVEMBER 2001

As we walk down the park road, I search the sky to get my bearings. On my boat, there's always a compass and GPS to guide me. But here, there's only the sun and my approximation of where the water is—the water being the Chesapeake Bay, which always tells me where I am.

The road ends at the South River, so I figure we must be heading north. Or is it east? I mentally map the contours of the park, searching for the river to determine exactly where we are. I'm becoming more and more absorbed in this little exercise when—at precisely the point where the shoulder between us and the road is at its slimmest—a silver sedan appears around the bend with a dog head protruding out of the back window.

It's hard to tell from this distance, but from the looks of the pointy ears and sleek head, the dog appears to be a Doberman. The car comes closer. It *is* a Doberman. As soon as the dog catches sight of Barney, he starts barking like a lunatic. Adrenalin pumps through my body. Within seconds, I'm in full panic mode. The car is a few yards away now, gaining on us fast.

Desperate, I pull Barney toward the trees, looking for an opening, but the thicket and bramble bushes are too dense; there's no way to make it through. By now, the dog in the car has squeezed himself as far as he can go through the window opening, all head and neck, a barking machine directing his fury at Barney, who looks in the direction of the car with mild interest. The driver of the car seems oblivious, which only increases my anxiety. What if the dog escapes, slips through the window opening? Leaps into our path? I can just see it: the blur of fur and teeth, two uncontrollable animals going after one another.

As the car moves past us, the dog stops barking and cranes his head backward to look at us. Barney begins investigating a low-hanging pine tree branch. I'm shaking. We've made it, but the encounter has me so rattled that I wonder if it's a good idea to keep going. Not many cars drive into the park during the middle of the week, but the ones that do usually contain canine passengers on their way to the dog park—often more than one. Some are well behaved, some are howlers, and some are absolute head cases like that Doberman. I am afraid of them all, afraid their owners will pull into the parking lot where my car is, walk where we walk, or let their dogs run loose even though there are signs all over the park stating: *Pets must be on leash.*

For the past few weeks, each time a car has appeared, I've been praying, *Keep going, keep going. Stay away from us.* And for the most part they do, heading farther down the road, toward the dreaded dog park at the very far end of the park. The Doberman affair is the closest we've come to an actual encounter.

The car with the Dobie disappears down the road. Barney takes the lead, unraveling the leash to its full length. "Barn, what am I going to do with you?" I say, talking more to myself than him. He swivels his head, acknowledging me briefly before returning his attention to yet another interesting section of pine branch. In the silence of the woods, my words echo back at me. *What am I going to do with Barney?* The better question is: *What am I going to do with me?* I'm the one who overreacted. But what if the Dobie did jump out of the car? My dog Sundance used to do that all the time. Things like that happen.

But it didn't.

With no car in sight, it seems foolish to turn back, so we continue toward the gatehouse. After we pass a thicket of pines and a deer path, another car appears. Once again, there's a dog in the backseat. I pull Barney in and try to put as much space between us and the road as possible. My neck muscles tighten as the vehicle approaches, but the dog, a sedate tan hound, quietly watches us through the window as the car passes.

When the hound is out of sight, we resume the walk, crossing a service road to a small hill where a young dogwood stands among a few smaller trees. Barney and I walk up the rise to get a better look at the little tree, which still has a nursery tag dangling from a branch. I tamp the loose ground around its roots with my sneaker just as Barney begins to lift his leg. "This tree's got enough problems," I tell him. "Give it a break." The sky is clouding up now, and for some reason it makes me afraid. The sapling is so exposed on this hill, I wonder if it will make it through the winter.

We turn back to the car. The wind picks up, and the crispness that first greeted us becomes raw as the sun hides behind the clouds. I pull my coat closer, worrying about that little dogwood. Walking beside the forest, I can see row after row of thin saplings rising from the forest floor, their varying sizes a testament to years of growth.

What makes me think the dogwood won't survive? Little trees make it through the winter all the time, enduring the cold to emerge taller and stronger when spring comes. What's that old saying? *What doesn't kill you makes you stronger.*

We continue down the road, Barney's ears flapping in the breeze, a big smile plastered across his face. It's odd, but walking into this wind—plowing through it head-on instead of cowering before it—I feel something warm and certain stirring in the deepest part of my being. I'm tempted to cross back to the meadow, but I don't. I let the leash out and follow Barney down the road. Just before we get to the car, the clouds break apart and the entire forest shimmers with light. Another car snakes toward us in the distance. I pull in Barney's leash like before, but this time I take a deep breath and keep walking as the car passes.

Two weeks later, we're walking next to a wildly contrasting forest. Some trees have reached their peak of color, while others are already stripped down to bare bark. It strikes me that trees are not so different than people, each one reacting differently to the same set of circumstances. Take the weather. Why do some trees go into shock when the temperature drops and lose all their leaves, while others hang on until the last minute and flame out in a blaze of glory?

While Barney sniffs a stubby patch of grass, I study the pale yellow leaves of a young birch at the side of the road. The leaves are tissue-thin, so transparent you can see right through them, and yet they cling sturdily to the branches, waving like paper lanterns in the breeze. If I were a tree, I would probably be like this one—small and thin, quick to react to the shock of cold, yet not willing to completely let go of the past. I'm pondering this, considering what it means to hold on in this way, when the sound of breaking twigs erupts from somewhere in the woods.

Immediately, adrenaline rushes through my veins. Gripping Barney's leash handle, I turn toward the noise just in time to see a small herd of deer running from us: three does and two little fawns. The babies follow behind the older deer, the white dots of their tails getting smaller and smaller as they bounce farther away into the dark of the forest.

As I watch them disappear, my heart calls out, *Come back, come back!* If only they knew there was no reason to be afraid of us, no need to run. Barney is never interested in deer, although anything smaller is fair game; and I'm so easily alarmed I could almost be their kin. I stare into the woods until no trace of them remains, still feeling a little wobbly from the residue of terror that had just coursed through me. As we continue down the road, the panic subsides, but not the thrill of what I've just seen.

We round the bend past the little dogwood and walk toward the gatehouse. This section of the park road has become part of our territory, a gray ribbon of asphalt unraveling a longer and longer thread of possibility at my feet. It's always Barney who pulls the thread off the spool, Barney in the lead, urging me on, constantly up ahead, giving me his *oh please* look when I want to turn back. Sometimes I feel like a turtle, slowly moving forward, stretching my neck a little farther each time.

When we get to the gatehouse, the safe harbor of the picnic meadow disappears at our back and another kind of meadow emerges: a sea of stiffened weeds and tall, drying grasses where a sign announces that we are in another country, ecologically speaking. We have entered the Wetlands Mitigation Area.

The openness of these scrubby lowlands has made this one of my favorite places to walk, not only because of the beauty but also because the tall grasses usually compel Barney to move his bowels, which is the reason I tell myself we are here.

With the wind blowing at fifteen knots, everything is alive with motion. The sea oats bow down as Barney and I approach, waving as if we were old friends or part of the family, which, in some ways, I suppose by now we are. I move closer, stepping onto the strip of grass bordering the road so I can listen to the wind moving among the brittle bodies. The sound I hear is language, an ancient and soothing tongue that bypasses verbal cognition and speaks directly to the deepest part of me. It's an old song, one I know I've heard before, but so long ago it seems like it was in another life.

Barney stops to dip his nose in a clump of dried weeds, giving me time to examine the silky tan and gray plumes atop the stalks. Words bubble up inside as I look at the grasses—*oatmeal, tarnished silver*—words pushed into being by these sea oats waving in the wind, by this day before me.

In the distance, the shrill scream of a police siren buzzes through the air, jolting me back to reality. Checking my watch, I realize I'm already late for work. We make our way back to the car on a road covered with leaves of all shapes and colors: deep maroon and blood-red maples, pale yellow poplars, delicate brown leaves eaten into lace, all so beautiful I cannot help but want to preserve them like I did when I was young. I pick up a red leaf speckled with gold spots and suddenly I'm nine years old, standing before an ironing board in my mother's bedroom waiting for the iron to heat up. Tree branches from the forest surrounding our four-room cottage scrape against the roof, while an old oil furnace clunks through the walls. My finger grazes the steel plate of the iron, pulling back from the sting of the burn, the heat that lets me know it's time to begin. Choosing one of the prettiest leaves from the pile, I sandwich it between two sheets of wax paper, place a towel over the paper, and press the iron down, waiting until the smell of the melting wax lets me know the sealing is complete. Then I place the waxed leaf between the pages of a book.

This is how I held on to what I loved. How a treasure was saved forever. Something is happening out here. I can feel it. Memories melt and merge, coming into clearer focus, becoming bright and vivid, lingering like leaves caught on a net of road.

When we get into the car, I tear a scrap of paper from an envelope on the floor and write about the sea oats and leaves and the dazzling mosaic of colors. Words begin to fall from me and I retrieve them, pressing them like leaves between two sheets of paper. It's as if I can't help but harvest the thoughts and images whirling in my head.

The scribbled notes on the passenger seat will not stay quiet. They chatter on and on in my head, refusing to be ignored. Writing has always been a part of my life—first as a child making up stories about happy families, then as a teen with poem-filled journals, then as a young songwriter penning lyrics about lost love. Later, the stories returned, written late at night and on the weekends, and then, not at all.

It feels good to write again, and not just write but to swoon over the consonants and vowels, to savor the rich feel of them rolling over my tongue. Maybe the words I thought were lost forever haven't disappeared but are simply waiting to be plucked like dried leaves on the forest floor—tinder for a fire that has never really gone out.

CHAPTER 4

THE SOUTHERN LOVE PUPPY

THE FIRST OF DECEMBER BRINGS A WARM AND SUNNY DAY, WITH temperatures climbing into the high fifties. As soon as the car turns into the park entrance, Barney presses his head between the bucket seats and leans against me as if saying, *Good choice, my friend—I'm with you on this one.* My eyes are fixed on the view outside the windshield, but when I glance over at Barney, his big grin smiles back at me.

I pull into the lot and park in our usual space near the meadow, making sure to attach Barney's collar and leash before letting him out. We head in the direction of the picnic tables, passing the hot coals bin, now blackened with the old ash of summer cookouts. Barney roots around in the grime, dusting his muzzle with soot, then looks up at me with that smile again, the same one that captured my heart so many years ago.

No matter where I am or how I feel, whenever Barney smiles at me a piece of light breaks off and enters my heart as joy.

When I first saw him, he was lost, a stray pup wandering loose in a Piggly Wiggly parking lot in South Georgia. I was lost then too, certain that

I had just made the biggest mistake of my life. Six months earlier, I had moved to Savannah, following my husband to a job at a small radio station just outside town. I hated living there, and I resented being forced to leave Arlington, Virginia, where I had felt at home for the first time in my life.

An East Coast girl at heart, I always felt landlocked in the Midwest, smothered by the hills and low cloud ceiling of the Ohio Valley. Moving to the Washington, D.C., area was like a dream come true. I loved everything about it: the big city vibe, the proximity to the ocean, the diversity, the culture. But shortly after we moved, the wall of panic I had kept at bay burst apart, unleashed perhaps by the uncertainty of the move or by the sheer pressure of being held back for so long.

They say you spend your twenties running away from your childhood as fast as you can, and your thirties slowing down and looking back at what you left behind. At thirty-six, what I saw when I looked back overwhelmed me. I began experiencing night terrors and insomnia and was plagued with obsessive thoughts centered on the fear of what *would* happen, not what was happening. If I momentarily forgot that the panic was going to be there when I set my head to the pillow, the thoughts would begin again, pressing down like a bully sitting on my chest. *Don't forget . . . don't forget.* It was a relentless system of mind control.

The insomnia got worse, accompanied by two recurrent nightmares. In one, my legs crumpled as I crossed a street, collapsing at the exact time the signal changed and the blazing lights of oncoming cars headed toward me. In the other, pale arms reached out from a grave and tried to pull me under.

It was the dream of those ghostly arms that scared me more than anything else. For the first time in my life, I felt desperate enough to consider the quiet bliss of no longer existing. Up until then, I was able to medicate myself with alcohol—vodka laced with cranberry juice, rum and cokes, or straight up shots of Peach schnapps. But now, nothing numbed the pain. Desperate, I made my way to a twelve step meeting, almost literally on my knees.

I'd been to meetings once or twice before, brought by friends and my own curiosity, but never understood the concept. People sat around and talked—so what? Nobody gave any advice. They spoke and they listened. It drove me crazy.

But the night that I attended my first Adult Children of Alcoholics meeting in a smoke-filled room above a camera store in Falls Church, Virginia, I *was* crazy. I had tried everything I knew of to stop my thoughts from spinning out of control but nothing worked. I was desperate for help, any help. This time I sat and listened as if a curtain had been lifted. Little by little, over several months, relief came from sitting among others and hearing their stories. Eventually, I began telling my own.

The program suggested I put my faith in a higher power, which was problematic since I had a hard time putting my faith in anyone or anything. But eventually, the guidance and structure of the twelve steps themselves became the "something greater" I could put my trust in. And it worked. I started to regain a sense of hope and a stronger, if fragile, faith in myself.

Then my husband lost his job. It took him a year to find another one, and by that time his frustrations, combined with my intense focus on recovery, began to take a toll on our marriage.

Curt and I were college sweethearts, although that sounds like a ridiculously old-fashioned way to describe our rock-and-roll relationship. We met in the florescent-lit studio of Full Moon Radio, the student-run progressive rock program that broadcast during the overnight hours on Cincinnati's public radio station. He was introduced as his radio pseudonym, "T.I. Duck" (the "T.I." standing for "The Illusionary"). Even with the weird name, when he turned from the turntables to say hello I was struck by how cute he was (just like Eric Clapton), but I already had a boyfriend then—the station manager who made the introductions.

It turned out Curt was a student in the broadcasting department at University of Cincinnati where I had recently enrolled after spending a long, aimless year trying to get my life together since returning home from California. And he wasn't just a disc jockey, he was also a musician and a film major, like me. Since the film department was small, we saw each other often and eventually started hanging out, spending long hours listening to music and having heated discussions about film noir, punk music, and the cinematic surrealism of Luis Buñuel.

Best of all, he made me laugh.

One day, Curt passed me in the hall as I was leaving dance class. At this point, we had been friends for almost two years. "Best legs in the broadcasting department," he said. I frowned at him and shook my head, but I couldn't deny that something was happening between us, a physical charge when we were together. Not long after that comment, we both gave in to the attraction we felt for each other. My friend became my boyfriend.

The chemistry between us was intense at first, and I fell completely in love. But it wasn't always easy. We lived together for four years, and in that time, he went on to become one of Cincinnati's top rock-and-roll disc jockeys. Women threw themselves at him, men bought him drinks wherever he went. Sometimes he would stay out until the early morning hours, leaving me wondering where he was and what he was doing. Still, I loved him and needed him. And my dog Sundance approved of him, which was the ultimate test. When he asked me to marry him, I made him promise we would leave Cincinnati someday. Reluctantly, he agreed.

Seven years later, Curt fulfilled his promise. By that time, he was established in rock radio and on top of his game. Leaving Cincinnati for a top ten market like Washington, D.C., was a big risk for him and it wasn't long before it became obvious the situation at the new station was not a good one. There were constant power struggles with his program director, who was threatened by Curt's newly created position as operations manager. The program director began a campaign to oust Curt, and, after two years, he succeeded. But as untenable as the situation was at the station, losing the job was worse. For the first time in fourteen years, not only was he unemployed, but he also was no longer the radio "personality" that had become his identity.

For one whole year, he sat around the house watching TV or spent evenings jamming with musicians he met at the neighborhood tavern. The job offers were few and far between, and never good enough. I was caught up in my recovery, barely able to keep going each day. On our twelfth anniversary, we sat across from each other in a Chinese restaurant and opened our separate fortune cookies. I wondered how much longer we would be together.

When Curt got the position in Savannah, he told me he was taking it whether or not I wanted to come. It was one of those times in a marriage where the road forks and you have to make a choice: either stay together or start down your own path. Even though I loved D.C., had a decent job, good friends, and resources to support me, I followed him as if in a trance, held by a connection that could not be severed and also by the unshakeable belief that I was not strong enough to stand on my own two feet.

For months, I stumbled through the South, filled with resentment for having to leave my home. Nothing was right there; the stores were too small, the weather was too hot, the people were sluggish and stupid. I wore all black in defiance of the Southern women's code of flowery excess, even though it made me a magnet for the heat. And even worse, I couldn't seem to find the kind of programs and counseling support I had up north. The panic attacks and depression still plagued me, although the small amount of recovery I had under my belt helped me deal with it, somewhat. Mostly, I walked around arguing with my newly found Higher Power.

One hot October afternoon, I stopped at the Piggly Wiggly to pick up something for dinner. I had left the store and was heading for my car when I heard brakes squeal and saw a black dog dart out from under the wheels of a pickup truck. Always a sucker for a dog in trouble, I ran after him, flip flops flapping on the hot asphalt. It was like trying to catch a pinball in motion.

When I finally caught up with the dog, he was in the middle of the road blocking a minivan from backing out. He was all black and as big as a full-grown dog, although he moved with the goofy, awkward gait of a puppy. There was no collar around his neck. I bent down and called, "C'mere, sweetie." His tail wagged enthusiastically. It was as long as his body.

The second time I called him, he walked toward me, all shining eyes and too-long legs and a lopsided smile that filled the entire lower half of his face. At first, I thought he was the funniest-looking dog I'd ever seen. But as he got closer and the smile got bigger, something melted inside me, softening like the tarmac under my feet in the blazing South Georgia sun. For the first time in a long time, I laughed for no good reason.

I coaxed the dog into the car and took him over to the neighborhood vet to find his owners. Neither the doctor nor anyone in his office had ever seen him before. They offered to take him to the shelter as a stray but I said no, that's okay. Secretly, I was glad they'd never seen him, glad he belonged to no one, because from the moment he smiled at me, I knew he was my dog.

When I brought him back to the vet's office the next day, the doctor guessed that he was about six months old and a Lab-Rottweiler, a mix that could result in hip problems, strong doggie odor, and skin allergies. As if to prove his point, the vet gestured to the rash on his belly, most likely a skin allergy. And with Rottweiler in him, he said, there was always the possibility of aggression. It seemed like the vet was trying everything he could do to talk me out of adopting the pup, but nothing could sway me.

Finally, the vet held up the pup's biscuit-sized paws and told me to take a look. "He's going to be big. Real big."

I had already noticed those paws. They were the biggest paws I had ever seen on a puppy.

"I like big dogs," I said. It was a bit of an understatement. My former dog, Sundance, was my protector and guardian. For two years, ever since he died, I'd been looking for a dog who could fill his paws. Sunny was a wolf-husky. This dog promised to be even bigger than him.

Within days, I named the pup Barney, after both Barney Fife, the bumbling deputy sheriff on *The Andy Griffith Show*, and Barney Rubble, Fred Flintstone's muscular, squat friend. I also called him "Lucky Dog," although finding him was lucky for me, too. Not long after he came into my life, I found a new job, wonderful women friends and, most important of all, the writing teacher who would become instrumental in coaxing out the words that put voice to what had been piling up inside me for a long time. Since there was no twelve step group for Adult Children of Alcoholics in Savannah, I started one, creating a support system that, while not exactly like what I had up north, was a good enough stand-in. Curt and I began finding our way back to solid ground. And there was Barney—funny, loyal, loving Barney.

Soon the rest of Barney's body began catching up to those big paws of his. He grew and kept growing, from forty-five to sixty, to eighty, then ninety-five pounds of dog and muscle at ten months of age. Without a fenced yard, Barney needed to be walked often, and as he gained in size and strength, our walks became a battle of wills. If he spied a cat or a squirrel, he'd pull me off my feet and drag me across the road like ballast. I was all of ninety pounds myself and no match for my muscular dog. But if trying to control his energy on a walk was a struggle, it was nothing compared to what was to come.

CHAPTER 5

DR. BARNEY AND MR. HYDE

AROUND BARNEY'S FIRST BIRTHDAY, I PACKED HIM IN THE CAR AND drove ten hours north up I-95 to visit my sister in Baltimore. The big city was baffling to him with its sidewalks and tiny plots of grass, so my sister brought us to a small park on the industrial side of the harbor. We strolled along the water, watching enormous container ships glide past while seagulls flew above our heads, surveying the area for fish and garbage scraps. Halfway through the walk, two boys approached, trailed by a big German Shepherd. The dog was not on a leash. The Shepherd ran past the boys and headed straight toward us, not stopping until he was next to Barney, exhibiting all the hallmarks of aggressive behavior—stiff tail, invasive sniffing, fur ruffling across his back. Barney submitted to being investigated, whining and nervously wagging his tail, unsure of what to do next. The tension in the air was palpable. I screamed at the boys, "Get your dog," but before they could reach us, the Shepherd lit into Barney in a frenzy of fur and teeth.

It took four humans to pull the Shepherd off Barney. Fortunately, there were no puncture marks, but there were scars. From that day on Barney was never the same with other dogs. He became the aggressor in all canine encounters, attacking before there was any chance of being attacked. My easygoing pup had become a clone of the animal who attacked him.

Veterinary behaviorists call dogs like him "dog-aggressive," attributing the behavior to a dominant alpha nature. Perhaps he was dominant—I always did seem to end up with the alpha males—but I was convinced his aggression was connected to what happened in Baltimore. Outside of this one quirk, Barney was the sweetest animal you could ever meet. He was gentle with babies, and he let little kids get away with murder. It was as if he was a lovable Lab with humans and a junkyard Rottweiler with other animals. Curt and I began calling him "Dr. Barney and Mr. Hyde."

Not long after the attack, we moved from Savannah back to the Washington, D.C., area, where Mr. Hyde began showing himself on a regular basis. Whenever we'd get too close to another dog on a sidewalk or bike path, he would curl his lips into a snarl, raise his hackles, and make it clear he was just itching for a fight. One day my sister brought her nine-week old puppy to my house, a darling German Shepherd named Arby. We decided to introduce the two dogs in the yard instead of the house where Barney might feel inclined to defend his territory. Stupidly, we forgot that a backyard is very much a dog's personal territory. As soon as Barney ran out, he made a beeline for the pup and immediately sunk his teeth into him, biting off a chunk of his tiny head. Arby survived, but with aggression problems of his own that my sister attributed to his traumatic encounter with his "cousin." A few months after that, a pet sitter opened the front door at the same time an unsuspecting elderly Lab on a leash walked past our house. Barney pushed right past the sitter and headed straight for the Lab, attacking before anyone could do anything. The sitter, her boyfriend, and a passing boy were able to pull him off before he could do any damage. Later, when I got home from vacation, the dog's owner called and asked if anything like this had ever happened before. No, I told her, because nothing *exactly* like that had ever happened before. But from that day on, I couldn't even open a door without making sure Barney wasn't around.

This was life with Barney. Everywhere we went I constantly had to scan the horizon for trouble. But the truth was, it wasn't much different from the way I'd been operating most of my life. Like him, the need for protection took precedence over anything else. We were twins, the two faces of fear walking side by side.

After living in northern Virginia for five years, Curt and I moved to Annapolis, a quiet harbor town on the Chesapeake Bay thirty-five miles east of Washington, D.C. This time, the move was for my job. I liked living near the Bay, close to the water and all the joys that came with it. But once more, I had to find places to walk where the chances of running into other dogs were limited. Barney and I sought out the empty spaces at the edges of town—wetlands clogged with beer cans and plastic bags, vacant lots littered with empty pint bottles, creek beds with syringes and soggy underpants washing up on their muddy shores. These were places of ragged beauty and muted violence. It wasn't the safest way to take a walk. But it was better than no walk at all.

By now, Barney accompanied me everywhere, even to the office where his sweet, people-loving personality made him the company greeter. On the way to work, we'd grab walks where we could, usually at an empty ball field near my home, navigating the glass-covered sidewalk and parking lot next to it. After one quick visit, Barney licked his paws obsessively all day. I was sure it was his grass allergy (as the vet had suspected, the rash he had as a puppy turned out to be a significant allergy problem that led to a lifetime of shots and pills), but when he got up, he was limping. I took him to the animal hospital, where they removed a piece of glass from his paw and handed me a bill for two hundred and thirty dollars. For weeks, I wrapped and re-wrapped his paw with gauze and tape. It was a battle to keep him from chewing the bandages off.

Not long after his paw healed, I took him back to the sidewalk near the ball field. Once again, he stepped on some broken glass and cut his paw. I cursed the idiot drunks who threw bottles out their car windows and cursed my own stupidity. I knew I shouldn't walk him on littered sidewalks and trash-strewn parking lots. Most of all, I knew I shouldn't look away, not even for a moment. But sometimes a cardinal would appear out of nowhere or a branch of blazing sumac would catch my eye in the afternoon light and I'd be gone. I took my beauty in small doses, stealing it whenever I could.

My mother couldn't understand why I refused to take Barney to the park. "It's so close to your house," she said. "Everyone brings their dogs there."

Which was exactly why I didn't.

The park *was* close, only a mile and a half away. Each time we passed it—to and from the grocery store, to and from the library—my mother's voice got louder and louder in my head. And the truth was I was tired of sneaking around with my dog. Tired of vet bills, of injured paws, and tired, too, of the long banishment in our little Siberia.

There are many ways to build fences. Fear is one of them. On the face of it, who wouldn't want to come to this park with its acres of woods, trails, and picnic areas; a visitor center resembling a Victorian mansion; and an amphitheater where people gather on warm evenings for summer concerts? Pet owners bring their dogs to the two dog parks (one for little dogs and one for big ones) and a dog beach on the shores of the South River. But it has been exactly these things that have kept me away—the people, the dogs, the woods—the unknown catastrophes I imagined happening.

In two months of walking here, there have been no catastrophes, nothing more serious than barking dogs sticking their heads out of cars. But on a cool November morning, while we're finishing up our walk, Barney stops at a pile of leaves under a sweetgum tree and begins rooting around in it. When he looks up, he's got a line of drool spilling out of his mouth. I bend down to rub the goop off Barney's muzzle and notice something, someone out of the corner of my eye. It's a woman walking down the park road with a dog beside her, both of them too far away for me to tell if the dog is on a leash. Immediately, the light mood of the previous moment is gone.

I pull Barney in the opposite direction of the woman and her dog, making a fast dash to the far end of the meadow and away from my car. As they get closer, I can see that the animal is leashed, but they are still way too close for me to feel comfortable about Barney's reaction. The woman turns and begins walking toward us. I feel trapped. If I go any farther, I'll have to walk into the woods. I tighten up the leash and pull Barney toward me. The fur on his back begins to rise. I'm standing there, bracing to rein him in, when at the last minute the woman and her dog turn into the footpath and disappear into the woods.

Relieved, I quickly head toward the car, hoping they don't decide to come back. Just before we get to the parking lot, Barney finds some garbage on the ground and crunches down on it. I stick my hand in his mouth but it's too late—only bits and pieces of bone float in the muck of saliva coating my fingers.

"You're disgusting," I say to him, wiping my hand on a clean section of grass. He smiles broadly as if I've just complimented him. My body is still tense from the close call we've just encountered, but the look on his face is so happy, so proud that before I know I'm smiling, too. We stand there at the edge of the lot grinning at each other like two idiots, which we are of course, and there's nothing I can do about that.

CHAPTER 6

WINTER 2002

THE WESTERN SHORE OF MARYLAND IS NOT EXACTLY SNOW COUNTRY; just the threat of two inches of frozen precipitation can trigger area-wide school closings. But last January, a blizzard descended over the Chesapeake region, dumping twenty-three inches of snow in a forty-eight hour period. As the snow fell and fell, I hunkered down in the house baking cookies and hoping that the power wouldn't go out. Finally, the storm drifted out to sea, leaving behind a shimmering landscape of powdered sugar hills and whipped-cream streets. Even though it was risky to go out (snow inevitably brought driveway-shoveling homeowners and their loose, frolicking dogs), after two days of being cooped up inside, I simply didn't care.

I hooked Barney up, swathed myself in down and wool, and took off past the snow-frosted wedding-cake colonials. The reflection of sunlight on snow was dazzling and the air was fragrant with the smell of wood fire curling out of brick chimneys. We walked past kids and shoveling neighbors without any problems until we almost reached the end of the street where a loose, snow-colored Samoyed appeared out of the whiteness and approached us with a friendly, wagging tail.

A woman stood nearby with two snowball-making children, boys no more than three or four years old. "Get your dog," I yelled. "Please." I yanked on the now immobile leash in an attempt to drag Barney away before the Samoyed could enter his circle of doom.

"It's not my dog," the woman called out. "But don't worry, she's friendly."

The Samoyed kept coming, getting closer and closer to us until her face was almost right up to Barney's. I pulled and pulled on the leash but it was too late. In a lightning instant Barney had her on the ground and tore into her. I yanked the leash hard so that his prong collar dug into his neck, but it didn't faze him. He attacked again and again, not stopping until blood trickled from her neck and I was finally able to drag him away.

By this time, a group of parents and kids had gathered in the snow-covered street. "She was loose," I pleaded. "There's a leash law in this county."

"You're supposed to control your dog," one woman said. Another pointed out that the Samoyed had gotten on her belly to show submission to Barney. "Any normal dog would have backed off."

The mother of the snowball brothers wanted to know where we lived. "We've got young children in this neighborhood," she said. "This dog is dangerous."

I told her no, no, no. He wasn't dangerous. He loved kids, even let my toddler nephews ride him. There was no problem with kids, just other dogs. *Really.*

They weren't buying it.

As we walked away, I heard one of the boys say, "Bad dog."

"Fuck you," I said under my breath, immediately feeling like a bad dog myself.

After that, any hopes of walking Barney in the neighborhood were shattered. He went back to being the invisible dog in the community, the half-Lab face hidden behind a fence or peering out of front room windows. His only view of the full street was from backseat windows fogged with dog drool.

But one year later, here we are, walking in snow just deep enough to make everything clean and new again with no loose, friendly dogs around—only me and the Barn. We make our way slowly across the snow-smoothed meadow, unblemished except for a generous sprinkling of prickly pods whose stemmed bodies look like spiked cherries on a vast vanilla sundae. A thin layer of clouds battens the sky, giving the light a reflective, dream-like quality. In the muted silence, the only sounds are those of my steps and my dog's as we sink through the thin rime to the powder below. Is there any better place to be alone with your thoughts?

I start singing out loud: "Sleigh bells ring, can you listen, in the lane snow is glistenin'. . . . " Barney wags his tail and smiles up at me. Although I'm sure he has no idea what I'm saying, he always likes it when I sing. We cross the road, where Barney pulls me toward a curving bank of snow, a round ridge of whiteness that reminds me of the igloos and snow tunnels I used to build when I was young. Staring at the slanting hill before us, I hurdle into the past like a child on a runaway sled. Suddenly, I'm outside the little house in the woods packing snow into hard, dense balls with my wet mittens, ignoring the burn of frost against my fingers.

At seven, eight, ten years of age, I couldn't get enough of snow. I'd shove it in my mouth, feel it melt on my tongue, sit on it, lie in it, make angel wings with my arms. Winter, spring, summer, fall, nothing stopped me from being outside—not the bitter cold of January or the caterpillars that hung from the trees like tinsel one spring or the seventeen-year cicadas that crunched like peanut shells under my feet. I found something to love in every season.

I'm struck by the sobering stillness of winter. The quiet cold is like an empty bowl, and my thoughts fill the space. Barney is too busy seeing, smelling, tasting, to ask anything of me except to keep going. *Look at this! No, over here!* He brings me back to the present, back to earth, which is a good thing for a person who has trouble staying grounded. We make our way down the road. The tree branches groan as a gust of frigid air blows into the park. I pull my coat tighter and keep walking.

At the sound of a car approaching, I guide Barney over the plowed ledge of snow on the side of the road where a barely visible trail leads into the woods. Barney pulls the leash out to wander a few feet into the path. But there are footprints in the snow—shoeprints, paw prints—so I head back to the main road again. The sun has broken through the clouds, throwing shadows at our feet—two feet following four feet, moving together as if in a practiced line of legs at the ballet barre, legs that seem to know where they're going.

I used to know where I was going.

Five years old. Walking six city blocks on my own to the high school auditorium to take ballet lessons. Standing on a stage under the harsh lights of a darkened hall where a tall woman ordered us to reach for our toes, which I did, easily, without bending my knees, "a natural," the instructor said. *Up, down, up, down* on those toes. Fingering frilly pink tutus in Bamberger's department store, imagining myself as one of the tiara-wearing ballerinas gliding across the stage during the New Jersey Ballet's performance of *Swan Lake.* There was no doubt in my mind as to what I would be.

But two years later, we moved to the country where there weren't any dance classes, or so I thought, until the day I saw a sign in front of a white farmhouse that said Martinsville School of Ballet. When I pointed it out to my mother, she nodded and kept driving. Week after week, back and forth to the post office, the grocery, home again, we passed that sign, never stopping. The future ballerina's stage was reduced to the wooden floors in front of the "hi-fi" audio system of our tiny living room, with most of the dancing taking place in my head.

My mother was a big fan of Broadway musicals and had an impressive collection of soundtracks from all the hit plays. I spent hours listening to show tunes, lifting the needle and starting songs over and over, learning every word to every song on the record. The ballet star dream was deferred to that of the star singer who prepared over and over for her solos in the elementary school choir. Turning up the soundtrack to *Sweet Charity* as loud as the Zenith stereo speakers could handle, I'd belt out "If My Friends Could See Me Now" along with Shirley MacLaine, seeing myself in the flapper dress, the glittery shoes, a long tapered cigarette holder in my hand. In my dream I had a voice, but in the real world I had no voice at all. I said nothing when the girls on the bus made fun of my clothes and how skinny I was, nothing when my father told me way too much about the "facts" of life, nothing when teachers in our rural school system singled me out in class for being Jewish. I was well practiced at having no voice by the time I made my way out into the world.

A person who has a fierce desire to express herself will dance around that desire all her life until she unleashes what is inside of her. As Barney and I walk in the snow, I think about how much I have frozen out of my life: first dancing, then singing, then acting, then filmmaking, and finally writing— much of it shelved in the service of staying hidden. Instead of being in front of the spotlights, I have ended up in the background, settling in a career as an arts administrator, hovering in the wings as what author Julia Cameron calls a "shadow artist," a person who helps others create while knowing that's the life they want for themselves.

On the back cover of my journal, I have pasted a line from a Mary Oliver poem: *Tell me, what is it you plan to do with your one wild and precious life?* Under that, I have taped a picture of a man diving off a cliff into blue waters. Tucked among the journal's pages is an article saved from a Sunday paper about a writing program at a nearby university. In it, a novelist who is a professor at the school says "I believe it is possible to lead a writing life."

As Barney and I trudge through the slush on the road, I consider the phrase *writing life.* The words imply a way of living that opens and doubles on itself like an origami flower, constantly revealing new dimensions. Once in the car, I jot down *look into grad programs* on a scrap of paper.

As we leave the lot, the tires slide unexpectedly over a patch of ice. I let them go where they want to, giving in to the loss of control—the only thing you can do in a slide. The car continues swerving to the right before reaching a patch of dry pavement beyond the ice. This is the moment I have been waiting for.

I straighten the wheel and head for home.

On a February morning, Barney and I head toward the picnic area, or at least where the picnic area should be—it's hard to tell. With the weather spiking into the forties, what's left of the snow has melted into fog and everything is shrouded in gray; even the air is thick with a shape and substance that plays tricks on the mind. A garbage can looks like a child, a shrub an animal. Trees float in midair, their trunks cut off from earth and sky by floating sheets of mist. "Just a short walk," I tell Barney. A few minutes or so and then we'll go.

Barney moves confidently ahead, savoring the smells marinating in the moist earth. While he pauses to sniff the ground, I gaze up at the roiling sky, losing myself in the swirl of mist and trees. Then I hear a noise, the sound of footsteps, close. Very close. Almost upon us.

Before I can even turn toward the sound, the ground disappears under my feet. Something grabs me from behind, choking me, squeezing the air out of my windpipe. I can't breathe. Can't move. Can't do anything. *I'm going to die. I know it.*

A tug on the end of a leash pulls me back into my body. The park is empty. Just fog and trees. Air begins moving freely into my lungs. The ground once again feels solid under my feet. I race back toward the car-shaped lump of fog in the parking lot, shove Barney in the backseat, and get in quickly, locking the door. My hands are shaking so badly all I can do is sit there and wait for my body to calm down. Outside, the fog drifts in waves across the meadow where a girl walks through the mist in patched jeans and a checked shirt, singing softly to herself.

The fog was already thick by the time I headed onto the streets of Berkeley to visit a friend. Along the way, I stopped to buy an ice cream cone. By the time I came out of the store, it had begun raining. Juggling the cone in one hand, the umbrella in the other, I walked down University Avenue and made my way to what I thought was my friend's street. The night was dark and moonless. Everything appeared fuzzy at the edges, half-hidden as if wrapped in gauze: sidewalks, houses, street signs.

I had only visited this girl once before, in the daytime. Now, at night, everything looked different. One block down, I turned onto what I thought was her street. But it didn't look right so I turned back, walking up to the intersection to read the street sign. As I attempted to make out the name of the street, I glimpsed a man out of the corner of my eye walking in my direction. He was a blip on the periphery of my vision, something noted and discarded as not important. I turned my attention back to the sign, squinting to read the words in the foggy darkness. The street name sounded familiar, so I crossed back over and went down the same direction as before, singing a Taj Mahal song in the rain: "Champagne don't make me crazy, cocaine don't make me lazy, ain't nobody's business but my own. . . . "

Nobody's business, not the night, not the fog, not the man on the corner who showed himself for a brief moment and then disappeared. I walked slowly, lazily, listening to the rich sound my voice made in the moisture-laden air. *Is this the house? This one?* In front of a two-story cottage, I slowed down and checked the house number. *Nope.* Continuing on, I tried to picture what this street looked like during the day.

It was beginning to dawn on me that maybe this wasn't the right street when an electric jolt of pain shocked my body. Someone or something was behind me, on me, squeezing my windpipe, cutting off my breath. I couldn't breathe. Couldn't think. I had no sense of where I was or what was happening except that what was happening was malevolent and all-encompassing.

My legs lifted off the ground, my whole body resting on the fulcrum of the vise-like grip around my throat. With my face tilted toward the sky, all I could see was fog and blackness. White-hot stars flashed in front of my eyes. Involuntarily, my hands flew open, releasing the ice-cream cone and still-open umbrella. The grip around my neck squeezed tighter. A voice in my ear said, "I've got a gun. If you scream, you're dead." I did not scream.

Now I knew exactly what was happening. I remembered what the police said to do in situations like this: *Cooperate. Don't resist. You'll only make things worse.* But even as I scrambled to try and save my life, I believed there was no worse. As the man dragged me down the street, I knew I was going to die, right here on this night in this place in this way. I thought of my mother, my sister, my little brother. I saw the face of my beloved grandfather. I grieved for them all, for their pain and their loss. I would be dead but they would have to live with the knowledge of what happened to me for the rest of their lives.

My attacker eased up some when he realized I wasn't going to put up a fight. He held me tightly, keeping the gun or whatever it was at my back as he shoved me down a dark driveway. "Don't scream," he said. "I'll kill you."

He was black, I could tell by the dark skin on the arm gripping me. *Don't scream.* I couldn't if I wanted to. I was immobile, incapable, an insect stung by the paralyzing venom of a spider.

For years, I will have dreams in which I try to scream but I can't. My mouth opens, my diaphragm contracts but nothing happens. It is nightmare that wakes me over and over. Only my voice can save me and I have no voice. No way to articulate the terror resonating within.

Desperate to get out of this alive, I made a conscious decision not to look at my attacker's face. Somehow, I believed if I didn't look at him, he would have no reason to kill me. Throughout the entire ordeal, he remained only a voice to me. But I knew who I was to him: nobody. Although in shock and completely disoriented, I recognized this with absolute clarity. As far as he was concerned, I wasn't a girl who loved to sing or a friend who baked cookies or a daughter who still missed her father. I wasn't even human. Knowing this was almost unbearable. It was a kind of death in itself.

At the end of the driveway was an old wooden garage with a car parked in it. The garage doors were open. My attacker pushed me onto the car and shoved his body up against me. He told me to pull my pants down. I heard myself saying, *Please don't. I'm a virgin.* This was a lie, but only a small one since I'd only been with one boy before in my entire life. There was silence, nothing at first. Then a demand, "I said pull your pants down, bitch." The next thing I knew, my insides felt like they were being ripped apart. Then I left my body and watched from above as a girl became a hole filled with emptiness.

Afterwards, the voice told me to pull up my pants. He grabbed me by the arm and pushed me down the driveway. As we approached the street, I heard a car door slam. Two people, a man and a woman, got out. My attacker wrapped his arms around my shoulders and whispered not to say a word. He still had the gun, he reminded me. "Walk with me," he commanded. "Just like boyfriend and girlfriend." The words sickened me. Still, I said nothing as we passed the couple and headed down the street. A few feet down, I saw my ice cream cone splattered on the sidewalk.

When we reached the corner, he let go of me and searched the pockets of my jeans, fishing out a twenty-dollar bill and a small baggie of pot. "Here," he said, handing back the pot. "I don't want to take your stuff."

Even then, still in shock and dazed by what was happening, I realized the absurdity of that statement. Didn't want to take my *stuff?* He had just taken everything.

Then he was gone, just like that, heading back toward the main street. Stunned, I stood there for a moment before running like hell toward my friend's house down the next street. This time, there was no doubt, no hesitancy. I knew exactly where I was going, guided by some internal honing system toward safety.

All I wanted to do was take a shower, to wash his hands, his semen, his crime off of me. I knew I was washing away "evidence." What did it matter? I had no intention of going to the cops. What could they do, anyway? My friend's friends—two young lesbian women who lived in the house—huddled on the sofa holding each other, their eyes wide with horror. Speechless, they watched and listened, looking as scared as I was when it all happened.

That night, I laid next to my friend, although sleep was impossible. My body and mind were racing, adrenalin pumping through me like water through a fire hose. The next morning, I made my way back to the tree-shaded carriage house I had called home in Berkeley. Within days, I moved across the Bay to San Francisco, crashing in a second-floor apartment with a bunch of Jesus Freaks.

Staring out at the meadow, I grip the steering wheel and try to focus on the present, to *breathe in, breathe out,* but it's no use. I was nineteen years old then, damned and determined to do what I wanted to do. The morning of my arrival in San Francisco, the newspapers announced that Patty Hearst had been kidnapped by a group calling itself the Symbionese Liberation Army. The Zebra Killer was still on the loose, a black serial murderer who left notes of revenge on his white victims. Danger was everywhere, any normal person knew it. But I was not normal. I was a girl who was running away from who she was and saw only what she wanted to see.

After the attack, I did not grieve. I did not cry. I followed the instructions of the doctor at the Free Clinic, soaking in a tub of warm water for thirty minutes each day to heal the raw wounds inside me. In the mornings,

I sat alone and rubbed a rosewood mala—a necklace of meditation beads—chanting *Nam-myoh-renge-kyo, Nam-myoho-renge-kyo*, six times, seven times, as many times as I could say it in the prescribed fifteen-minute period. It was a Buddhist chant that was supposed to make good things happen. Day after day, *Nam-myoho-renge-kyo*. I had no idea what the words meant.

If a person walked toward me, even on a crowded street, my body stopped in mid-movement, ready to turn and run. I no longer hitchhiked to job interviews. I took the bus. When I walked in the fog, ghoulish fingers wrapped around my shoulders. I only walked alone in daylight if I could help it, and not very far.

Not knowing what else to do, I stuck to my plan, starting a band with some musicians who had recently moved to town from Pennsylvania. We practiced in the living room of the bass player's Swedish girlfriend until we could play through entire songs without stopping. I kept chanting on my beads for good things: gigs for the band, a job for me. On the surface, it all seemed fine. Nobody knew what had happened. But if I had to wait for a bus on a lonely street corner, my body filled with so much fear that it literally shook. When I smoked pot, my mind ran in circles, filled with paranoid thoughts. In my dreams, I ran on wobbly legs from faceless pursuers. When I woke, I'd find myself gasping for breath.

After two months, I gave up on waiting for good things to happen and asked my mother to send me money for a plane ticket home to Ohio. From my window seat, I could see the mountains and dust-sprinkled plains I had driven over on my way to California. What I had loved most about the West was the way the sky and land went on forever—wide, open, with nothing to hold you down or hold you back. Now the very thought of being so exposed terrified me. My great ambition was whittled down to one overriding desire: to make sure that what happened to me would never happen again.

CHAPTER 7

THE FOUR-LEGGED CRUTCH

Before leaving for California, I had gotten a wolf-husky puppy, a striking black and white boy with one brown eye and one ice blue one who was to remain in Ohio with my mother until I could send for him. When I left, Sundance was a tiny thing. But upon my return I was greeted by a six-month-old, thirty-pound monster who terrorized the entire family.

One afternoon, not long after I came home, he grabbed a piece of bread from my little brother and ran under a table. When I stretched my arm out for the food, he snarled at me, threatening to bite. I had owned dogs all my life, but never one who had challenged me like this. I pulled back for a moment and then stuck both my arms under the table, dragging the snarling ball of fur out by his two front paws. He growled and bared his teeth. But I did not back down. It was the first time since the rape that I had it in me to fight back and it felt good.

In order to control this dog, I knew I would have to learn to become an alpha female in our pack of two. I went to the library and read up on wolf behavior and took my lessons back home. When Sundance's eyes meet with mine, I stared back and refused to look away until he did first, the wolf equivalent of throwing in the towel. I kept my voice low and force-ful when commanding him. I was fair but firm and, over time, I gained his respect and loyalty. It was a small but significant step in regaining my own respect.

Sunny accompanied me everywhere—in the woods, on my walks, and when I moved out on my own. Obedient up to a point, he could still be obnoxious beyond belief to others. Since an alpha lets her inferiors head out into the wild and do the hunting work, there was no good guidance on keeping this dog contained, and Sundance was a master escape artist. He could climb garden walls and slip through a cracked door. He hurled himself through screen windows and shimmied under fences. He took his freedom, but he gave me loyalty and protection in return. He was my body-guard, my guardian, the keeper of my solitude.

When Sundance got loose and ran away for days, when he robbed little old ladies' shopping carts or brought back unopened bags of dog food stolen from back porches, I shrugged and said I couldn't control him. But perhaps what I really couldn't control was my need for him to embody all that I wasn't. Sundance was my alter ego, a force roaming the streets with teeth unfurled, stalking and threatening anyone who got in his way.

Little by little, I got my footing back. With Sundance by my side, I was able to step out into the world again. I went back to school, majored in filmmaking, fell in love with the cute, funny boy who spun records at the campus station. After years of living together, we got married. But having a husband didn't lessen my need for Sundance. Curt worked the evening shift at the radio station, which left me fending for myself at night.

It was Sunny who was beside me when I walked the streets at night, Sunny who accompanied me to the country to sit among the trees and clouds. Sunny who helped me feel safe.

With a husband, friends, and a companion the local hooligans called the "devil dog," I managed to be fairly independent, at least on the surface. But the shadow of the past walked with me wherever I went. If I came home at night and had to walk from the car to the house alone, my heart pounded until the door shut behind me. If I went to the gym or the mall or a meeting at night, fear stalked me all the way through the parking lot. I armed myself with awareness, heavy keys, fast steps and, when at all possible, Sundance.

As the years went by, Curt became well known in town, while I fought to find my own identity as his wife. He was perfectly happy being a big fish in a small town, but the restless urge to leave Ohio still stirred in me. When Curt received the offer from the station in Washington, D.C., I was overjoyed.

By the time we moved east, Sundance was almost twelve. He still seemed as vital as ever. I think it was impossible for me to see Sunny as anything but strong, even after he began stopping to catch his breath on our nightly walks. When he developed powdery welts on his belly, his vet recommended a canine dermatologist in western Maryland, a specialist who had more experience with this kind of thing. She took one look at Sundance and diagnosed the rash as cancer, the welts very much like the Kaposi's sarcoma lesions of AIDS. Her advice was to return to his regular vet and have X-rays taken. If the lesions were evident in his lungs, there was nothing more that could be done.

The very next day, I took him for the X-rays. In the darkened office, the vet flipped on the light behind the film, revealing a chest riddled with splotches of white. The cancer had spread throughout his body. I crumpled with grief at the news.

"If this was my dog," the vet said, "I know what I would do."

I didn't know what to do. All I knew was I felt like I had fallen into a hole with no bottom. On the way home, I stopped at a small park. Sundance walked only a few feet before stopping, as if too tired to go any further. Then he raised his face to the sky and tilted his head back, smiling at the sun. My heart broke just looking at him. I couldn't do it anymore. I couldn't handle knowing he was going to die. I brought him back to the vet and held on to him as he took his last breath.

We had a backup dog, Curt's sweet white Shepherd Sasha. Her presence was a comfort. But although her size and shepherd looks were enough to give someone pause, she wasn't the protector Sundance was. As much as I tried to connect with her, I was a one-dog woman, and Sasha was not that dog. When I lost Sundance, I lost a piece of my freedom. I wasn't sure I'd ever find another dog like him.

For two years, I grieved for Sundance, carrying my sorrow in my heart and his hair in a locket. It was the second time that death had swept into my life and taken away someone I loved.

It didn't make it any easier.

CHAPTER 8

MARCH 2002

MARCH COMES IN NOT LIKE A LION BUT LIKE A DRUNKEN BEAR, stomping through the Mid-Atlantic with wind gusts of up to thirty-five knots, knocking down power lines and snapping tree branches as if they were twigs. In the park, I stay close to the tree line, grateful for what shelter we can get from the windbreak. As we walk, I hear odd sounds in the woods—soft, baleful moans, and groans that sound like rusty hinges on a swinging porch door. It takes a while to realize that what I'm hearing are trees being pushed to the edge of endurance by the wind. Above us, a pine sways back and forth, releasing a mournful sound as it bobs toward the earth. It's the sound of grieving, a sound that calls me back to my father.

No matter how much time has passed, no matter where I am, the first of March is always the same day: the anniversary of my father's death. The memory remains encased in ice, as fresh and real as if it is still happening. The calendar turns, February ends, and there I am on the front steps looking down at my father lying on an icy patch of driveway next to the open door of his still-running car. Exhaust hisses from a hose stuffed through a small crack in the driver's side window, a hose that snakes all the way back to the muffler. My mother stands next my father's body, screaming in her high soprano wail for him to wake up while I stand there, barefoot on the cold slate, wearing a flimsy yellow bathrobe covered with tiny flowers, the helpful daughter who has no idea how to help this time.

I was fifteen then, a child on the verge of becoming a woman, old enough to know that my father was in danger of falling, but young enough to believe it would never happen. And yet when it did, when he finally went through with what he had threatened to do for so long, I was relieved. Saddened and shocked and splintered, but relieved. The winds of his rage stopped blowing through our house on that day. I naively believed that was the end of it. What did I know?

March is a bully, just like its namesake, Mars, the Greek god of war. I don't trust it, not any of its thirty-one long days of gray skies and brutal winds. Even when it's warm, its cold, a cruel tease throwing in a few spring-like tidbits before taking them away again. As I walk with the wind at my back, I realize the entire year before my father died was like one long March, days upon days of sadness and fear broken up by bright days of hope. It was a relief when my father died, but only because the fear of what might happen stopped. The pain did not. I loved my father more than anyone else on this earth. He was a funny, thoughtful, wise man who could also be cruel and abusive when driven by the winds of depression and mania.

After my father's death, my mother gave away all of our furniture. She had me go through his closets and drawers and put all his things into big cardboard boxes to be picked up by Goodwill. I remember standing in his closet, breathing in the smell of him, trying to pull the essence of who he was into me so that I would never be without him.

My father used to say there were always at least five solutions to any problem. To elaborate this point, he'd set up a little question-and-answer game for me based on hypothetical situations. "What would you do," he'd ask, "if some kid at school was bothering you—you know, calling you names?" I hated this question. There were a group of girls on the school bus who were always "mocking me out" and I usually did nothing. "I could call them names back," I said.

My father nodded. "That's one solution. What's another?"

"I could tell my teacher."

"How about number three?" And we'd go on and on until I scraped out five things I could do, even if the last were silly answers, like saying I could just stand there and cry. As I cleaned his closets and packed away his life, I wondered why, if he knew there were always at least five solutions to any problem, he picked the one he did.

Among the groaning trees, Barney and I make our way toward the gatehouse. As we walk, clouds race through the sky, big puffy things like lambs without feet. They collide and merge and break apart and merge again, opening up the heavens and covering them up again as the winds of winter clash with the winds of spring. In a most elemental way, I am watching how change happens. And I realize the same kind of battle is going on within me.

Last month, with great trepidation, I requested applications to two graduate writing programs. When the fat little packages arrived in the mail, both wanted to know the same things: *What are your expectations? Your writing goals? The reason you're seeking a writing degree?* I dug down deep inside to answer them, judging each word with torturing scrutiny, editing and revising right up to the deadline. As soon as the applications were finished, a new set of questions emerged: *What if I'm rejected? What if I'm accepted? Where am I getting the money?* And the scariest question of all: *What the hell makes me think I can do this?*

My father used to tell me his goal was to be a millionaire before he was fifty. Instead, he killed himself at forty-nine, one month shy of his fiftieth birthday. I am almost as old as my father was when he took his life. Applying to grad school has unleashed the unsaid fears of my father's legacy—*Don't bother, you'll never be able to do it. Don't try, you'll get hurt. Don't dream. You'll end up like him.*

If I listen to these words, nothing will ever change.

For dogs, there is no self-questioning, no second guessing, no five freaking answers; there is only the immediate present, the Buddha-like ability to be with what is and to respond appropriately. While I curse the wind and hug my coat closer, Barney pushes forward, ears blown back, head high to sift through the scents blowing his way. A faint smile curls on his lips, and he seems energized by the weather, taking on the headwinds like the gutsy tank of a dog he is. Nothing stops him.

Just before we cross over to the parking lot, Barney stops to lift his leg on a cherry tree. I notice small, almost imperceptible nubs pushing through the satiny bark on the branches and move in closer to get a better look. They're buds, or at least the beginnings of them. I run my gloved fingers over the bark, amazed at their stubby resiliency. The weather is still cold, unpredictable, but it doesn't stop the buds from acting on faith that the right conditions will ultimately prevail for them to bloom. It takes tremendous courage to anticipate good things in the face of adversity. It's humbling to see how brave these buds have to be in order to become a flower.

Later in the month, March throws one of her curveballs: a deliciously deceptive day, seventy-six degrees and sunny. On the way to the park, I detour to the post office to mail the applications for graduate school. We stop at a light, and I roll down the windows to enjoy the warm air. Next to me, an old gray SUV idles with a bare knee poking out the open window. Coconut-scented suntan lotion wafts in the air.

Barney tilts his nose toward the window as we enter the park. By the pond, cherry trees explode with starburst clusters of pale pink flowers against dark wood. The Bradford Pears are in bloom, their white popcorn crowns puffed into the shape of a Jiffy Pop sack.

I park the car in the playground lot, where a ring of bright yellow forsythia blazes in the sun. Overcome with light, the outline of the branches disappears and only the blooms shine forth like brilliant yellow stars in a ground-level sky.

I feel drunk, cut off from the earth, crazy with sun and blooms, with my applications flying off like whirly-gig seeds seeking the right ground to root in. I cannot do anything at this point but lose myself in the carnival before me. The ground is softening, unexpectedly early. It's still March, sure, but why not be hopeful? All around, beginnings are unfurling their promise.

CHAPTER 9

SPRING 2002

T.S. ELIOT SAYS APRIL IS THE CRUELEST MONTH, BUT IN MARYLAND it's not as cruel as it is cranky. When Barney and I get out of the car, a cold, light rain spits out of a sullen sky. It's not pretty, but it is quiet—no cars, no people, no dogs. This is the saving grace of crappy weather—it keeps most everybody else away.

We head toward the forest by the picnic area and follow the tree line. Even though the foliage is minimal, it acts as a pretty good rain break. The precipitation reaching us is reduced to sheer moisture, soft and sponge-damp against the skin. I grab a fistful of hair for a quick frizz check. It's damp and fuzzy. "Great," I say to Barney. "Already a bad hair day."

I can't wait for this walk to end. I'm worried about my hair, about being late for work, about this bad weather that looks like it's about to become worse any minute. "C'mon Barn," I plead. "Gimme some action."

Reeling his leash out so he can find an irresistible spot to unload his business, I wait for results. No luck. Barney noodles through the underbrush as if we have all the time in the world. When we reach the place where the footpath cuts into the woods, I let him start down the trail, allowing him to go in as far as the leash will take him, but don't follow. When he's forced to stop he looks back at me with pleading eyes.

Ever since the first day we set foot on this meadow, he's been trying to get me to walk onto this path, and I've refused, afraid of what I might find. But as I stand there, the rain picks up and the path looks so dry and comfortable under the umbrella of new spring growth that I move forward into its shelter. Immediately, I'm covered by a gauzy tent of trees, safe and dry. I take another step in and then another and, before I know it, I'm walking down the path with Barney in the lead.

Barney immediately puts his nose to work, rooting out some smelly thing under a pile of dead leaves. I turn to the forest, waiting for him to move on, and become aware of a crinkling sound, like the crunch of wrapping paper in a fisted hand. It grows louder, then softer, then louder again. I'm not sure what it is, although I'm certain it's not human or dog, and because of that, I'm able to listen in a completely open way. As my ear becomes attuned to the subtle tone and pitch, I hear what sounds like shifting sheets and cracking bones. A small shock of awareness shoots though me as I realize it's the sound of the ground waking up.

I move forward in a trance, following Barney deeper and deeper into the woods. The meadow disappears behind us, and Barney takes on the posture of a hunter, his ears up, tail perky and aimed for the sky. If he were a person, he'd be yelling *Ya-hoo!* As it is, he dives right in and takes the lead, nose to the ground all the way.

What is it about this place? The hush? The singing rain? Or is it the way the two exist in the same space? My steps slow down. Time becomes fluid, evaporating entirely, and I take it in, all of it—the rain, the soft crackling, the trees standing like uneven rows of shutters. Certain that no one is around, I breathe deeper, giving myself permission to not do anything but just be here. I forget about my keys and my Mace and the need to be aware. My legs feel strong, my mind uncharacteristically devoid of thought. The path turns lightly and then begins to descend. I'm scanning this new vista to make sure the coast is clear when something on a tree catches my eye, and in that split second, before my brain can register what it's truly seeing, the image of a girl tied to a tree flashes before me: *Charlee.*

Charlee was a girl I knew in high school who ironed her hair and cleared up her acne and transformed herself from plain old Charlene Weiss into a sixteen-year-old version of Cher. She was hair-flipping cool, distant and quiet, a loner who lived in a small house on the corner of a working-class street. Boys flocked to her, while girls whispered that she was "loose," a slut, a girl who screwed around indiscriminately. Then one day she disappeared. Her parents were frantic, but everyone at school figured she had just run away with a boy. Two weeks from the day she disappeared, a hiker found her in the woods in Kentucky—raped, dead—propped up against a tree like a rag doll.

When it happened, I was shocked, but I saw no connection to my own life, even though we were the same age and went to the same school. I wasn't "loose." I didn't "give out." I tried to forget about it, but Charlee kept appearing periodically. After graduating high school, I began hanging out with a bunch of hippies who lived around the corner from the bar where she was last seen. The bar was a dark shotgun joint on the corner of McMillan and Vine, barely big enough for a pool table. Although I never went in, the door was often propped open, and from the street I could see stringy-haired men playing pool in sleeveless muscle shirts, and smell their vomit and beer through the open door. I imagined Charlee sitting at the bar, her long black hair hiding her face. I didn't see myself anywhere in that picture until what happened to her almost happened to me and Charlee took on new meaning: a warning, a red flag, a stop sign on an untraveled road.

Usually, just the thought of Charlee is enough to make me turn around and get the hell out of wherever I am. But this time, I finger the Mace in my pocket just to make sure it's there and keep going. A few yards farther down, a clearing comes into view, and then a beaten path leading to the second parking lot. I let out a sigh of relief. We've made it through the footpath, at least a part of it. It's such a small distance, really—I don't think we've gone more than two hundred yards from the meadow—but to have walked into the woods, to see Charlee but not be stopped by her—feels like a monumental achievement.

We step into the lot, into the light, leaving the dark canopy of woods behind. As soon as we reach the center of the clearing, the rain begins falling harder. "Alright, Barn," I say, "Let's go for it." I run and run under the liquid sky with my dog at my side, no longer worried about hair or anything in this moment. Before I know it, I'm laughing, feeling a little like a child and a lot like someone very much alive.

Weeks later, I'm at work, crunching budget numbers while Barney lies on the floor next to my desk, deep asleep as usual. The phone rings, and to my surprise it's a professor from the writing program that has already sent their notice of acceptance. The letter has sat on my desk for a week waiting for a response.

"Congratulations," she says. She asks if I have any questions.

Questions? Sure, I have questions. But I don't ask the one I really want to know: Why did they choose *me?* My mind races as we talk—*Were they desperate? Not enough applicants?* I stare out the window, aware of a whole family of Mexican jumping beans bouncing inside me. All this wanting, all this waiting, all this fear that I would not be accepted, and I don't know what to do. The fact that they want me throws everything off balance. Surely something must be wrong with *them* because they accepted *me.*

"So can we expect you to join us?" she asks. At first, nothing comes out of my mouth. Then, to my surprise, I say yes.

As soon as I hang up the phone, I squat down and rub the inside of Barney's ear with my palm. He leans his sleepy head into my hand. "Can you believe it, Barn," I whisper. "Can you believe it? I'm really going to do this." He looks at me blankly, until I say the magic words. "Want to go for a walk?"

There are times when my body cannot hold the thoughts inside it and the only thing I can do is put it in motion, the best motion being a walk. Since it's the middle of a workday and there's no time to go to the park, our choices for walking are limited. My office is located in the heart of a colonial-era town with uneven cobbled sidewalks that are far too narrow to allow Barney to pass another dog without a confrontation. Whenever we walk here, the first thing I do after the door shuts behind us is look both ways to make sure no one is coming. Then I cross the street to a safe stretch of sidewalk with no driveways or open spaces for a dog to pop out from.

After making sure the coast is clear, Barney and I cross the street. It's a lovely May afternoon and plenty of other people are out enjoying the warm weather. As we approach the intersection, I slow down to avoid being blind-sided by someone walking a dog just around the corner. Holding Barney back, I crane my neck and look around the bend. There's no one there. We turn. So far, so good.

But as soon as we round the corner, a torrent of barking explodes on the street. There's no dog in sight. There is, however, a silver BMW parked on the corner with a frenzied boxer in the backseat. The dog is ballistic, flinging himself against the window and barking so hard he keeps falling back into the seat. Before I know it, Barney drags me over to the car and claws at the window. The boxer fights back, furiously pawing through the glass. It takes all my strength to pull Barney off the car. Finally, I get him back onto the sidewalk.

Moving away from the still-barking dog, I notice a long line of scratches on the door's metallic finish. *The boxer started it,* I say to myself. *Serves him right.* I lead Barney away from the damaged car, teetering between feelings of guilt and righteousness.

We walk around the block and pass the hospital without running into any other dogs—in cars or out. As we approach the postage stamp of a park at the end of the street, I slow down to make sure the coast is clear. There are known problems here—an old Golden Retriever who lives behind a loose slat in a fence bordering the park and a couple of yipping Westies on the other side—but this green space next to the water is such a treat for both of us that it's worth taking chances.

Barney pulls me toward the creek's edge, magnetized by the sound of the lapping tides. He loves water even though he has only been in it once in his life, when we were on vacation in the Florida Keys. I walked out into the shallow surf and called for him to follow me into the ocean. Reluctantly, he dipped his paws into the milky water and then swam and swam, his inky black fur striking against the pale turquoise sea. He was barely a year old. Soon after, he encountered the attacking Shepherd and became unreliable around other dogs. I couldn't risk letting him loose to swim.

There have been many times since that I have watched other retrievers go after tossed sticks thrown into the water—in ponds, canals, even this very creek sparkling before us—while Barney could only stand on the shore, watching from a safe distance. We walk along Spa Creek with its slight tang of salt and fish, and I think back to my dog swimming in the clear waters of the Florida Keys, how beautiful he was moving in that sea. The wake from a passing boat laps up against the creaking wood pilings. Barney snaps his head at the sound and scans the waves, his duck-retrieving instincts intact. It saddens me to see it. A dog should do what a dog is born to do.

So should a person.

Friends and family find my choice to go back to school incomprehensible. I already have one advanced degree, and my job doesn't require additional formal education. A *writing* degree? I can see it in their eyes. What the hell do you do with that?

Someone asks me what the game plan is for the writing. I don't have a game plan—I can't even think beyond the first step, which is to get my butt into the classroom and start moving toward becoming who I am. *Becoming who I am? What kind of cockamamie, New Agey–type goal is that?* It's not a bigger car, it's not more money, it's not a second home. But it is a first home; a coming home. A claiming of lands that have been taken from me.

At forty-eight, I'm in this one alone. Even my dreams think I'm crazy. Homeless people keep showing up while I'm asleep, stealing my wallet, a part of my brain, my job. I dream of a man living in a sewer who has taken my purse. "I'll give it back when you have a book," he says.

On the way home from work, we stop at the park. A cold front is coming in, and the air is moving fast. I want to be in the movement of the wind, to let something bigger carry me along. The act of committing to the writing program has put me smack in the middle of two frontal systems. The strong one is fear—challenging my defenses, pushing me back to what I know and where I've been. Then there's hope—a weaker front, but insistent and enduring.

I'm elated. I'm terrified. Going back to school is salvation. It's tens of thousands of dollars I don't have. It's a door opening to my deepest desires. It's a lot of work. *I can't,* I tell myself. *I have to,* I say.

I put my back to the wind and allow myself to be pushed forward by force, by faith, by something I have no name for. My hips, my legs, my feet move forward, forward. The wind manipulates my limbs. *This is how you do it. Like this.*

Turning to go back, the force of the gusts push against me, but I'm determined to move ahead. *I will do it,* I say to myself, to Barney, to the wind slapping my coat below the knee. The headwinds pound at me, but I stay on course, resolved to continue on in the direction I need to go. *I can do this.* By the time we get to the car, it's obvious that the winds of resistance are not as powerful as they seem.

And I am not as powerless as I've let myself believe.

CHAPTER 10

SUMMER 2002

Ah, summer. Soft, warm, and sleeveless. Just the way I like it. As Barney and I walk down a shaded stretch of park road, the trees bend over our heads in slow, green waves. Breathing deeply, I try to capture this moment: the blue sky, the sweet air, the dog at my side. In less than an hour I'm to leave for the residency portion of the writing program, so this will be our last walk together for quite a while.

Kneeling beside Barney I try to explain what's about to happen. I'll be gone for two weeks. He will be spending his days roaming the house instead of going to work with me or exploring the park. "I'm going to graduate school," I tell him, the words sounding as strange to my ears as they must seem to his. Of all the dogs I have ever had, Barney is the most literate. When I say, "Go get Curt," he gets my husband. When I say, "Gimme a kiss," he kisses me. But when I say, "I'm going to graduate school," he looks at me quizzically, the "going" part of the sentence clear, but not much else.

We walk through the meadow to the south side of the park and cross the road to an access path leading to a trail so close to the road, yet so hidden it stunned me the first time I realized it was there.

About a month ago, we were walking along the tree line of what I had assumed to be a dense wooded area. Barney nosed around the tangle of vines and ground hollies while I daydreamed. Suddenly, a flash of color appeared through the trees, followed by voices and two joggers in shorts not more than thirty feet away. As soon as I realized they were on a trail, I pulled Barney back and ran toward the road.

Over the next few weeks, Barney and I shadowed this trail, peeking through the trees as if they were the gate of a secret garden, peeling off toward the road if people or dogs appeared in view. Like a careful research student, I mapped the geography (swamps, sticker bushes, poison ivy), the sociology (bikers, runners, strollers), made mental notes of the busy and quiet times. Most important of all was the discovery of two mown access paths leading from the road to the trail. Located on the north and south end of the trail, these offered the possibility of passage in—and, more importantly, out—if necessary.

It doesn't matter what the commitment is: an unknown trail, graduate school, a job with benefits. I can only enter in if I know there's a way out. The irony is that once I commit, I'm in it for the long run. I've been married longer than any of my friends. I stick with a difficult project until it's done. I keep dogs even when they are problem children. I am not a quitter. That's why taking the first step is always such a terrifying proposition.

But this is a day of first steps. Maybe that's why, for the first time since the discovery of the trail, I walk directly into the south access path leading to its entrance. We're so close to the trail that I can feel its shaded coolness. From here, it's apparent that the paved walkway is narrow, maybe five feet across; not nearly enough space to keep a dog out of Barney's hit zone. But rather than turn around, I reel the leash in and keep Barney close to my side. The coast looks clear. No one on the left. No one on the right. *What the hell,* a voice in my head says. *Do it.* And boom, we're in.

Immediately we're surrounded by a canopy of trees. In the uppermost branches, birds call to one another *fee, fee-be.* The air smells of earth and old memories. Webs hang on the underside of leaves, glinting in the sun as if holding secrets in their gossamer nests.

It reminds me of the first time I plunged into the underwater world of a Florida coral reef. My husband and I had gone out in a small boat with friends to go snorkeling. One by one, my companions fitted themselves with masks and fins and dove overboard, leaving me in a small, rocking boat surrounded by a turquoise-green sea. Ten minutes went by. Fifteen. The boat rocked, rocked, rocked, my stomach lurching back and forth with each movement. I lay down and looked at the sky. I took sips of Coca-Cola. I still felt nauseated, and then, more nauseated. Finally, I couldn't stand it. I slipped my feet into child-size fins, slapped on a bright yellow mask, stuck the plastic breathing tube into my mouth, and jumped into the water, where I floated on my belly and looked through the rectangular mask window. Phosphorescent parrotfish wriggled less than five feet below me, their luminous skins of red and orange and green gleaming in the sun. A school of soldier angelfish marched by, tiny yellow and black striped bodies flashing among the coral. Purple sea fans waved as if moved by the wind. At that moment, I didn't care if I did drown and die. Why live without seeing such a thing? It was the first visceral experience of understanding how much I had missed by being loyal to fear.

Nausea pushed me over the edge that time. Now the discomfort rocking me is subtler and the intention is clearer. The memory of the sea pushes me forward. I am a diver again, moving on a current of desire.

We pass the swamp pond, which I've seen many times from the road. From that limited vantage point, the pond appeared to be of hardly any size at all, but here, on the backside of the trail, it resembles a small, dry lake filled with dust and leaves. For a moment, I consider adding it to my mental topography as a possible exit in case we run into trouble, but then I notice ruts of black muck and change my mind. Like everything else here, there is a sense of mystery and power to this pond. I don't doubt there might be just enough moisture left to suck me and my dog into its depths.

The trail curves. Bends. And at each turn, my nerves kick up. We pass the swamp and enter a section where the path diverges from the road, and the woods and underbrush thicken. It would be impossible to leave the trail here. *Keep going, keep going,* I tell myself as I let out Barney's leash just enough so he can move out to where the Virginia creeper and poison ivy spill over the pavement. His excitement is evident, sniffing this leaf, that bush—in the moment, as always, a luxury I can't afford. I look around us with an eye for breaks in the wood where we can pull off if a dog appears around the bend.

Then, a strange thing happens.

I am more curious than afraid.

A two-story orange building looms through the trees on the opposite side of the trail from the road. It looks like a barn, or maybe a barn-like garage in the back of a house. We move on. More backyards appear, back porches, backs of houses bordering the trail. Small footpaths emerge, winding from the trail to fenced gates of the houses. The little paths and the houses give me a sense of relief, providing not only a buffer between Barney and another dog but also a sense of not being so alone here.

We pass a yard where someone has built a tiki hut–like structure with a huge brick barbeque pit. Brightly colored flags hang from the rafters, ragged from exposure to the sun and wind. I remember walking in the park earlier in the year and hearing a live rock band from somewhere in this general direction, most probably from this yard. An *ah-ha* feeling of satisfaction bubbles up inside as the topography fills out, the sociology fits in. I picture the band playing under the hut, the aging boomers swaying to Bob Seger covers, the sloshing plastic cups of beer. And then I picture a dog—the one barking right now, in the present moment, somewhere up ahead on the trail.

I reel in Barney and pull him over toward a house, bracing myself for the worst. We wait. Nothing happens. We wait some more. A voice calls a name. I hear panting, the scramble of feet up some stairs. A door slams. Then nothing. Just the birds. Another *ah-hah*. A yard dog. We move on past a sea of leafy pachysandra.

At the next bend, the trail takes a turn away from the road, and the space between the houses widen. A dead log, stripped of bark, saw-toothed and shaped exactly like a shark catches my eye, as does the small footpath next to it, leading from the trail to the road. For a moment, I think about ditching out, but Barney has already moved on beyond the path, so I follow, gently pushed by another current of wave. I decide to name this cutoff the Shark Trail and make a note to look for the shark if I need a quick exit.

Beyond this point, the woods thicken into a landscape of bramble bushes and impenetrable vines with no visible escape route. My stomach clenches.

After we round another bend, a wooden fitness station appears on the right with a sign that reads *Number 16, Pull-Up,* accompanied by an illustration of a generic human form in a pull-up position. With its bent knees and curled fists at chest level, the figure looks more like it's praying than doing a pull-up. Not that I'm big on praying, but at this point it seems just the right exercise to get through this dense patch of trail.

Finally, I see the sun breaking through the trees, painting a dappled mosaic of light across the trail. We're almost at the strip of mown grass connecting the north end of the trail to the road. We've made it—gotten through without a loose dog or a strange person or the shadow of anything at all. I'm as elated as if we've crossed a finish line. Barney and I exit off the trail and walk out into the bright sunshine where the heat shimmers in waves above the asphalt and graduate school beckons before me like an oasis.

The first week of residency the heat is relentless. I spend my time alternating between air-conditioned classrooms and a blistering hot campus littered with the excavated earth of summer-break construction projects. I walk past the same building site each day—from the dorm to the classroom to the cafeteria to the dorm and back—walking, walking, covering as much as or more ground than I do in the park with Barney, except on sun-scorched concrete and brick pathways lined with chain-link fence and traffic cones. It isn't lost on me that, like this school, I am now under construction, building a new foundation for myself. When the renovation is completed, this campus will be beautiful, an academic haven with wide green lawns and fieldstone buildings. But for now, it's all dirt and rock, a desertscape offering little shade except for the woods ringing the college—a cool, green buffer that beckons to me like a siren song.

One morning, I walk behind the campus where the lawn meets the woods. I follow the line of trees, taking comfort in being close to the forest. Occasionally, a footpath appears, but I cannot step into it, cannot bring myself to enter into the woods without Barney at my side. I feel disconnected, banished from the relief of solace and solitude by my need for safety. And this time, I can't hide behind Barney, can't say I won't go in because of loose dogs. A dog would be a welcome surprise. It's the threat of two-footed creatures that keep me away.

After one week, the heat, the pressure, the ground-breaking confusion is all too much for me. On our only weekend off, I get in my car and drive back home to my husband and my dog. The next morning, I wake to take Barney to the park and the cool confines of the Shark Trail. I need to walk it again, prove to myself that I have traveled strange and frightening territory before and that I can do it once more.

Parking the car under a shady tree, I open the door, leash Barney, and let him out, enjoying the feel of his fur under my fingers as I fix the collar around his neck. Before we head out, I lean down and thump the top of Barney's broad head with my hand, feeling less and less anxious with each satisfying *thwack*. It's as if simply by touching him, his calm is transferred to me. No wonder I take this dog to work with me. If only I could justify him as a therapy dog, I'd take him everywhere.

As we walk, I think back over the past week, of the strangeness of being back in an empty dorm room after twenty years absence; the comforting, musty smell of a cool basement classroom; the curious excitement as copies of essays are shuffled my way. Learning is a luxury. I knew that already. What I did not know was how much of a challenge becoming a writer would be.

During the first workshop, a critiquing session, my precious story was torn to bits, gently but thoroughly by my fellow classmates. Afterwards, I walked behind the cafeteria and sat on the curb trying to catch my breath and my thoughts. Workmen were renovating a nearby dormitory, the air filled with the rat-a-tat of nail guns and whir of power saws, echoing the cacophony of feedback ringing in my head. I knew the other students weren't trying to be cruel, but I felt decimated, worthless, exposed as the shitty writer that I told myself I was. A tight knot of tears gathered in my chest, but instead of crying I stared at the woods across the street while my fingers ripped at weeds at the side of the curb.

After a few minutes of mindless tearing and ripping, I looked at the torn pieces in my hands and recognized the familiar three-leaf pattern. *Poison ivy.* Now I'd done it. Found a way to really screw up my time here. I envisioned walking around campus with a puffy face, eyelids swollen shut, my skin covered in angry welts. I got up, careful to keep my hands from touching my body, and rushed into the communal dorm bathroom where I scrubbed my hands with Jean Nate after-bath splash (the only thing I had with any alcohol content). Then I walked over to the cafeteria, lemony-fresh and resigned to my fate.

What a week.

From somewhere behind us, a bicyclist calls out "On your left," bringing me back to the trail and to Barney, who has stopped in the middle of the path. I pull him over to the right where a wicked patch of poison ivy grows on the side of the trail. This park is full of the stuff, but since I'm wearing long pants, socks, and shoes, I'm not worried. Here, I anticipate trouble; I'm fully prepared to protect myself. On that curb, and in the classroom for that matter, I didn't even think in those terms. Who knew poison ivy grew between cracks in asphalt? Or that you're so completely naked when you read your work to others for the first time?

Miraculously, days after the plant-ripping incident, my skin is as clear as if it had never touched the ivy. I study my palm, the one not holding Barney's leash, and think about this sensitive skin of mine, how it can redden from simply touching a plant or bruise from a too-firm touch. I'm so fragile, so full of sensitivity, so full of precious bullshit. When criticized, I criticize myself worse. When rejected, I react with self-pity and anger. The last time I sent out a story and it was turned down, it took three years before I sent another one out. If I want to get anywhere in this world, one thing is for certain: I have to stop being so thin-skinned.

Barney and I continue on, following the backyards of homes bordering the trail. My eyes fix on the tarmac before us, and I remember how, as a child, I would begin each summer walking barefoot on painfully soft skin until the bottoms of my feet thickened and I could run and play without shoes on almost any surface. I think of Barney, how the bottom of his paws are so calloused from walking on all kinds of surfaces that they're almost burr-like in places. This is how the sole and the soul grow skin: by continuously walking over rough territory.

I get in the car and head back to campus just in time for Sunday dinner in the cafeteria. Grabbing a plate of mushy, oversauced pasta, I tell my dining companion, Rhonda, that I just don't see how I'll have the time to do the work. Rhonda is a second-year, a wise and seasoned senior in the program. She grabs a brown paper napkin from my tray and writes in big letters: *You can do it. Give yourself the time.*

"Read this whenever you doubt yourself," she says. I tuck the napkin into the inside flap of my notebook and carry it with me for the rest of the residency. When I go home, I tack it to the corkboard next to my writing desk. Then I take my mother to breakfast to break the news to her that I won't be able to spend as much time with her as she likes. Since her move to Maryland ten years ago, she has come to depend on me for her social life. Now there will be no more shopping together, no movies.

"The workload is tremendous," I tell her. "I have to read ten books. And write fifty pages before the end of the semester."

"That's awful," she says.

"I won't be able to spend a lot of time with you."

I watch her push a piece of egg onto her fork. She takes a bite, then looks me straight in the eyes. "You should quit."

Quit. I think of my father, the person who showed me what quitting really meant. And now this, from my mother, who obviously finds my using my time for myself unthinkable. I start spinning into a downward spiral of anger and disbelief. And then I stop. This is the way it's always been. What did I expect?

"I'm not going to quit, Ma."

Back home, I read and re-read the ragged lettering on the napkin on my board: *You can do it.* As the message sinks in, I step back from my mother's words, from my father's actions, from my own pained and restrictive reactions.

I turn on the computer and begin to write.

CHAPTER 11

RANDOM ACTS

CAN'T SLEEP. THE WORDS CIRCLE THROUGH MY MIND LIKE A MANTRA as I drag myself out of bed, slap on some makeup and get my dog into the car. By this time, it's almost noon and I'm sleep-deprived, overcaffein-ated, and thoroughly disgusted with myself. *Normal* people get up in the morning, even if they have slept badly. *Normal* people accomplish things by lunchtime. *Normal* people don't obsess that their life is going to hell just because they wake in the middle of the night. The announcer on the radio drones on, a blur in the background until a live news report breaks in, crackling with urgency. This morning, while I've been sleeping—or trying to—four fatal shootings have taken place in a two-hour period in nearby Montgomery County.

The details are sketchy, but this much is known: all of the shootings have occurred within a ten-mile radius of the I-495 Capital Beltway surrounding the Maryland suburbs of Washington, D.C., and all witnesses report a white van speeding away from the scene of the crime. The victims appear to be random—a retired schoolteacher mowing a lawn in Rockville, a cabdriver pumping gas at an Amoco station, a housekeeper waiting for a bus outside

Leisure World, and a suburban mom vacuuming a Dodge Caravan at a Shell station. The police think the deaths may be related. But it's too early to tell.

In the park, I lock my car and leash Barney, trying to remain as alert as possible on three hours of sleep. I force myself to straighten up, hoping my posture and stride will make someone think twice about messing with me. But even with Mace in one pocket and my big ring of keys in the other, at 5'2" and just under one hundred pounds, I'm well aware it wouldn't take much to take me down.

After our walk, the day unwinds like any other. I go to work, take meetings, and return home without any major somnambulistic screw-ups. There have been no reports of shootings in the area since the morning massacre. Then at 9:15 P.M., a seventy-two-year-old carpenter is killed by a single bullet as he walks across Georgia Avenue in Northwest Washington, one mile from the Maryland state line. Every media outlet in the District converges on the site.

That night I can't sleep again, though it's not the sniper keeping me awake. I'm terrified this latest bout of insomnia will spiral into the paralyzing anxiety attacks that have accompanied it in the past. I practice yoga breathing, then switch to tensing and relaxing various body parts, then, giving up on that, change positions (many times) before getting up to visit the bathroom (many times). Finally, I count backwards from two hundred. When I reach one, I'm still awake. And twice as frantic.

The next day, as Barney and I walk down the park road, squirrels rush through the leaves, gathering nuts as if nothing has changed. A hawk glides through the sky and swoops over a distant patch of wood. I think back to last summer when a Chihuahua puppy was picked up by a red-tailed hawk right in its own backyard. It seems no matter where you are there is always a vulture circling in the clouds. Just this morning, a woman was shot by an unseen assailant while loading packages into her van in a parking lot in a Michaels craft store outside Fredericksburg, Virginia. Police believe the incident is connected to the Washington-area shootings.

Fredericksburg is fifty-two miles south of D.C. on I-95. I do the math. If the sniper is willing to travel fifty-two miles south, surely he will think nothing of traveling thirty-five miles east.

Barney noses around a pile of ashes on the ground near a picnic table, hoping to get lucky with the remains of a summer cookout. "Cut it out!" I yell, pulling on his leash. He looks up at me, his graying muzzle smudged with a mustache of soot. I bend down to rub off the ashes, but before I can even get my gloves off the sound of gunfire echoes in the distance. My heart pounds against my eardrums. The sound repeats, sputtering this time, followed by a loud rumble. "Just a truck," I say to Barney, louder than necessary.

We head over toward the meadow, which is only a chain-link fence away from the main road. Walking in the open like this while a nutcase is on the loose is not the smartest thing to do, but it feels empowering—a way of pushing back against the hidden and uncontrollable forces that threaten me. It's as if I'm throwing up a dare to the gods of fate. *Come and get me, see if I care.*

Two days later, with the shooter still at large, I'm no longer so brave. I stick to the interior of the park just in case someone decides to take potshots through the fence. The leaves fall, creating space where there was none, and I can't help but see it: the summer leaving, the fall coming, the sniper out there somewhere but not here. In my chest, the soft hammering of panic is beginning its silent journey to the center. As we stroll past the gold-leaved birches, I am being taken down, slowly, deliberately, and the shooter is so well hidden I don't even know it's happening.

This is how it goes. I'm walking under a blue sky watching three geese soar through the clouds when a thought erupts like a bullet pulling a bird from the sky: *Remember,* it says. That's all it has to say. It's a trigger. Click. What I remember is panic, hopelessness, the fact that I cannot sleep, cannot dream, cannot stop myself from falling into the endless well of fear at the center of my being. The blue sky fades. The black clouds return simply by remembering them.

As we walk in the park, a warm breeze shakes the first leaves of fall from the trees. Squirrels scramble across the forest floor, foraging, fighting, chiding and chasing each other, but they exist in a far-away echo, something happening on the periphery of the hole I have fallen into. I can no longer hear anything but my own thoughts, stuck in the groove of a bad phonograph record, repeating . . . repeating . . . repeating. . . .

Still, life goes on. I go to work, keep up with the reading and writing assignments for graduate school, cook dinner for my husband, and take care of my dog. At night, I retreat to the computer, where, under the bronze gaze of Ganesha, Destroyer of Obstacles, words fly out of my fingers creating an essay about my father and the year leading up to his suicide. Sometimes the memories are too intense, and a scene lived through words can crack my heart wide open, unleashing a flood of grief and tears.

Patricia Hampl has said "to write one's life is to live it twice." I know that's true because after decades of blocking my father out of my mind, I see him wherever I go. At times, it's as if he's talking to me. There are other voices too, the ones that tell me I am insane, that I will never hold another job, that I will never sleep again, finish my graduate work, or do anything I want to do. As the voices drone on, I show up for work during the day, keep up with my writing at night, and chat pleasantly with my classmates online. No one suspects a thing.

Meanwhile, the sniper has hit again. A fifty-three-year-old man is killed while pumping fuel at an Exxon station off I-95, twenty miles north of Richmond. The police put out a sixty-mile roadblock along the interstate, but call it off after six hours. Once again, the sniper has vanished from the scene. Two days later, six miles west of Washington, D.C., a forty-seven year-old female FBI analyst is shot dead in the parking garage of a Home Depot near a Michaels craft store.

One entire day goes by without a shooting. Then another. For five days, it's as if the sniper has driven off the Beltway and out of our lives.

Almost overnight, the park quiets as fall descends on eastern Maryland. The chorus of cicadas dwindles to occasional solos. Bird chatter is softer, less frequent. I can't help but notice it, even with the constant chattering in my head. I see small things: the green leaves of a birch tree fading, the gradual shades of yellow. Spider webs, opaque on a gray day, shimmer radiantly when the sun comes out. Nothing stays the same. Not for long.

As we walk, I imagine the sniper cruising down Hillsmere Drive right outside the park. Barney tilts his nose into the air, blissfully unaware of all the turmoil going on in the world. How wonderful it would be to be a dog, living fully and freely in each moment.

I bend down, touch the slick blackness of Barney's fur, and bury my head in his neck. Simply by touching him, I'm comforted, soothed by the soft movement of his ribs as he breathes, the raspy panting as he stands to catch his breath. I love this dog more than I love anyone or anything. But who am I fooling? Barney isn't free. He's a prisoner, leashed and chained whenever he leaves the house. If he were free, he'd be all over this park. If he were free, he'd be able to ignore me when he turns in the direction of the woods near the playground and I say, "No. We're not going there."

He hears the weakness in my voice, the "no" that is less a "no" and more "I don't think so." He stops, plants his feet in place, and refuses to go any further. The sight of him standing there with his big Lab-Rottweiler head pointed longingly toward the woods makes me want to cry.

"What the hell," I say to the clump of grass at my feet. I turn toward the sound of children shouting and follow Barney's lead. We pass through the buffer of woods and reach the playground without incident—no dogs, no snipers, no random acts of any kind—just leaves and trees and nuts falling off the branches.

A whole week goes by without a sniper attack, and the entire region holds its collective breath, waiting for the inevitable. I stay glued to the radio and television, listening to police news conferences several times a day, tracing my finger over maps in the newspaper that detail each death by location and date. I search the highways for a white van, the kind servicemen use, the vehicle that always seems to be present at the scene of the crime. Like everyone else around here, I want to be able to do something to make this madness stop.

At 8:00 in the evening, a thirty-seven-year-old man is shot in the parking lot of a Ponderosa Steakhouse approximately seventy miles south of the Capital Beltway. This is when it becomes apparent to me that whoever is doing this is not a foreign terrorist but one of us, a red-blooded American who appreciates the subtle pleasures of a sizzlin' steak, Texas toast, and an unlimited salad bar. *An inside job.* The words resonate in my head. *Inside.* I'm beginning to understand in a way I never have before that this terrifying panic, this remembering, this thought prison of mine is an inside job.

Somewhere deep in my psyche, there is a terrible angel that wants to keep me safe so desperately it will lock me up in hell if that's what it takes.

By week's end, a cold front blusters its way into the region, arctic air fighting with the receding southerly front. The winds blow a steady twenty knots, gusting to thirty-five at times. As Barney and I head to the parking lot after a short morning walk, we're almost knocked over by a rogue wave made of air. I turn my back, stumble before getting my footing again, then hunker down into my jacket and wait for it to pass. The wind howls. Everything in its path bows before it, including me. In that moment, I know I am powerless against the winds that rage within me. The thought is strangely freeing.

The next day, the police confirm the discovery of a four-page note found in a plastic bag nailed to a tree in the woods adjoining the Ponderosa parking lot where the last shooting occurred. It consists of rambling, cryptic passages that address the police directly. The sniper writes: *Your children are not safe, anywhere at anytime.* And we know they are not; he has already tried to kill one of our children, a thirteen-year-old boy on the sidewalk in front of his own middle school. We are dealing with madness here; we all know it, and still, life goes on.

I take Barney to the park, reel his leash out, and watch his sleek Lab body wiggle in three parts as he walks ahead of me. He has always walked this way, the front quarters moving independently of the middle ribs, which move independently from his hindquarters. My heart sinks as my eyes fall on the inward-facing hooks of the prong collar jiggling around his neck. After years of trying harnesses and leashes, it's been the one thing that has stopped his runaway pulling and given me some amount of control over him. He doesn't seem to mind the collar, even waits patiently as the prongs are hooked around his neck. To look at him, you'd think he's a happy-go-lucky guy, not a canine bully with an anger management problem. But what kind of life does he really have?

I watch him lick a wet leaf, his entire being focused on the texture and flavor of what is most likely dog urine. When I murmur his name, he circles his tail in happy response. As we walk on, I ponder my question. *What kind of a life does he have?* A good life, I decide. A life with a woman who knows exactly what kind of beast he is and still loves him.

Maybe it's time to see myself as clearly as I see my dog. Perhaps it's possible to be inherently flawed and still have a decent life.

A day after the note is found outside the Ponderosa Steakhouse, a man identifying himself as the sniper calls the police. The call is traced to a pay phone at an Exxon station just off the interstate outside of Richmond, Virginia. Police descend on the area in force, zeroing in on a white van idling beside the pay phone. Two men, both undocumented immigrants, are taken into custody. They are found to have no connection to the sniper and are turned over to the Immigration and Naturalization Service. Meanwhile, the killer is on the loose, the elusive white van still swimming among us.

How does it happen, this seeing only what you want to see? I think about all the changes I've been going through: starting graduate school, cutting back my hours at work so I can write, worrying about money to pay for school and, perhaps most importantly, the impact of unlocking memories of the past in order to find story and meaning out of what has happened. All these changes, all taking place in fall, a time when even the slightest breeze can tip me over. Barney squats over a shrubby young pine and I hear myself say, "No wonder I'm going insane." It makes me laugh, and then the wind begins laughing with me, tickling the tulip trees, which in turn release their burden of leaves.

That's when I know it's time to leash this crazy dog running wild inside me. For years, I have gone on and off of antidepressants, taking them only as an act of last resort and only for as long as it takes to get out of the hole I periodically fall into. Medication is my prong collar, the thing that keeps my inner beast contained. I hate to do it, but when the depression takes over, it's the only way that I can get up and walk into my life again.

A day after the sniper's phone call, I'm awake, tossing and turning in my bed. At 5:56 A.M., a bus driver steps out of his Metro bus in Aspen Hill, Maryland, and breathes in the cool morning air before beginning his route. A single shot rings out from the direction of the basketball court across the street, landing in his chest, making him the tenth fatal victim of the sniper.

The following day, the police release a statement alerting the public to be on the lookout for a dark-colored Chevy Caprice with New Jersey plates.

The white van, the one we have all been watching for, turns out to be a red herring. For weeks, we have all been looking at the wrong thing.

In the early morning hours of October 24th, a truck driver sees a car fitting the description of the Beltway Sniper's vehicle at a highway rest stop in western Maryland. He calls the State Police. Thirty-three minutes elapse before they arrive on the scene to awaken and arrest two men sleeping in the car. One is a teenager with a Caribbean accent. The other, a tall, solemn man, says nothing as he is cuffed and taken away.

Following the arrest of the snipers, we learn many things. The Chevy Caprice had been sighted repeatedly at the scene of the shootings, but law enforcement officials chose to ignore it. The shooters concealed themselves in the trunk of the vehicle and shot out of a small hole cut into the rear tail-light of the car. The snipers were black, not white as suspected. The tall man was in a custody battle with his wife, who lived in the Washington, D.C., area and shopped at Michaels craft stores. Talking heads discussed possible motivations: revenge, money, power, insanity.

In my head, elevated levels of serotonin begin putting out the brush fires sprouting between the synapses in my brain. As the medication kicks in, the obsessive thoughts become quieter, and as the days go by, quieter still. I sleep at night for a few hours, and then a few hours more. When I write about my father, I can see all of him without falling apart. Things begin to return to normal, whatever that is.

One week after the sniper has been caught, the park is alive with color. Clouds float by, taking on the benign shapes of fluffy cartoon characters. Back in the car, I reach behind me and rest my hand on Barney's blocky head, grateful for the quiet miracle of loving and being loved without having to say anything. We sit for a while like this, watching squirrels run from tree to tree. Then I open the windows and let the soft breeze enter.

CHAPTER 12

FALL 2002

WITHOUT GLASSES, I SEE FARAWAY THINGS IN FUZZY, ABSTRACT terms—faces without features, signs made of squiggly lines. What looks like a can of peas on a supermarket shelf could just as easily be soup or beans. As school gets underway and the essay about my father starts to take shape, it becomes apparent to me that my writing is just as fuzzy as my eyesight. The writers I admire the most make their words come alive with descriptive language so vivid and detailed that I can see, smell, and hear what they are writing about. Feelings dominate on the page when I write—the swirling emotions arising from the internal conversations inside me—the interior life, not the concrete, sensory one that exists outside of me. My challenge is to start directing my gaze outward and learning how to articulate what I see there.

The inspiration for how to do this comes on a fall afternoon when the leaves are so full of color they blaze into small bonfires in the sun. Holding a maple leaf in my hand, I force myself to look at it over and over, to find new ways to see it, describe it: peach-colored here, pumpkin-orange there, red on the edges, a small gray spot ringed with brown. The veins feel hard and sharp against the soft flesh of my fingers, the little bumps near the bottom like poppy seeds that have been glued in place. I close my eyes and run my fingers over the leaf, reading its bumps and veins as if they are Braille, finding story in each tactile discovery.

Suddenly, it becomes clear to me how to move out of the cocoon of feelings and thoughts I've been living in for so long. The five senses—all of them—will lead me out of myself and to the words I've been seeking to write about the world.

Holding the maple leaf in my hand, I begin reviewing the senses: *sight . . . sound . . .* I get that far then blank out. Starting over, I focus on the corresponding parts of my body to help me remember. Eyes: *sight.* Nose: *smell.* Ears: *sound.* Lips: *taste.* Hands: *touch.* I count them off on my fingers again to make sure all five of them are covered: *sight, smell, sound, taste, touch.*

We walk a few feet down the road before Barney stops to sniff a pile of leaves. *Smell.* I take a deep breath, inhaling a moist, rich scent drifting up from the ground: the smell of earth. What does earth *smell* like? Closing my eyes, I breathe in the fall air as if it's a fine wine. It smells dank and damp, layered with the fragrance of musk and rotting fruit.

Moving on to the sense of *sound,* I concentrate on listening, really listening. Songbirds are chirping, a squirrel shuffles through the forest, a fire truck siren howls in the distance. Satisfied, I move on to the next sense, but I've already forgotten what it is. Like a blind person, I grope the contours of my face to find my way back to where I was, touching eyes, ears, nose, before resting my fingers on my lips. *Taste.* Running my tongue over my teeth, I try to distinguish a flavor of some sort, but there is none. Maybe this is what an empty mouth tastes like. *Nothing.*

As we round the bend, a car door slams. Immediately, alarm bells go off through my body. My eyes seek out the parking lot just beyond the meadow where a young woman opens the back door of her vehicle to take out a stroller. Once I realize it's just a mother and her baby, my body immediately starts to calm down. I'm frustrated with myself, aware how this reaction is automatic, my sensory receptors hardwired to panic at the slightest sound that could be a person. It's as if my senses have been hijacked. I don't listen to what is there; I listen for what *might* be there.

Barney and I continue down the road toward the parking lot. *Focus,* I tell myself, but by this time, I've lost track of what sense I'm on. I place my fingers on my eyes and begin again: eyes for sight, nose for smell, ears for sound, lips for taste and now . . . *touch.* I feel the touch of my hand against the hard plastic housing of the retractable leash, the cool air against my face, the solidity of the road under my feet. As I look around, and reclaim each sense again, I'm amazed at how much more there is to see, hear, smell, feel, and taste. Each sense is a ladder rung leading directly to the present. Every time my senses are activated, I am brought back to my body, back to the park; back to here. *Here.* With all that is.

A professor at school recommends reading Diane Ackerman's *A Natural History of the Senses.* I devour the descriptions of each sense, thrilling to discover the layers of experience found in taste and smell and sight and touch and sound. When I read that smell is the one sense that sends a message straight into the limbic system without processing it through language or even thought, I want to shout *Hallelujah.* Now I know why the smell of burning brush transports me to piles of live oak burning in the driveways of Savannah, or why each time I breathe in diesel exhaust I'm ten years old, walking past a bus belching smoke onto the streets of Newark, New Jersey.

At first, my only goal is to strengthen my writing muscles. But it's hard to ignore that something deeper and more important is happening. By exploring my environment and translating it into the language of the physical, I am learning how to inhabit my body.

The walks are not merely walks, but an exercise in living through the senses.

What am I seeing? What am I hearing? What am I smelling? What am I tasting? What am I touching? This is what I ask myself each time we walk. For brief periods of time, I can hear the rustle of leaves blowing across a field and not flinch, or watch the light flicker through the trees without wondering if I'm seeing someone move. I practice just being with what is, instead of reacting or processing it all through a filter of fear and safety.

In this way, I slowly begin to enter the world again.

And let the world enter me.

CHAPTER 13

WINTER 2003

BY FEBRUARY, MY TOLERANCE FOR COLD WEATHER ALWAYS REACHES A breaking point. Each year, I try escaping to warmer climes, but more often than not winter follows me. In Jamaica, the northwest winds incite the sea to madness, whipping the waves into ten-foot walls of destruction. Barbados isn't much better, sunny but windy, with that angry, frothing sea. Bahamas, cold and again, windy, the water uninhabitable. *It was nice the week before,* the locals say. Also, this, in island patois: *When de northwest winds blow up north, dey always end up here.* They don't tell you this in the brochures, that the Eastern Seaboard is a crap shoot in winter, even in its most southerly reaches. So this time, I decide to go far, far, south. Curt and I book a trip to Tobago, sister island to Trinidad, so close to the equator that it is practically a suburb of Venezuela.

The day we leave, the headlines are about the weather—the coldest winter the Mid-Atlantic has seen in years. I attempt to leave Barney's blanket and bed at the kennel, but they refuse to take it, saying they only use their own bedding. He appears anxious as they take him away and I'm so nervous leaving him that I back into a stone wall on the way out, embedding the car's bumper with pockmarked dents.

Tobago is pretty, warm, but with moody, often cloudy weather. We discover that our hotel is on the "windy" side of the island, where gusts of cool salt air keep everything in constant motion. Dogs are everywhere, feral, abused, abandoned, some of the worst treatment I have seen in the Caribbean, where, overall, dogs are treated like lepers or worse. At a food court near the beach I share some meat patties with the stray dogs hanging around the perimeter. The locals glare and yell at the dogs to go away when we turn our backs.

We go to the beach but rarely swim; it's just a little too cold. A few days into our trip, Curt shimmies down a beachside embankment and slips halfway down, spraining a finger as he reaches against the rocks to slow the slide. Within days, it balloons to double its size. Just before we leave, I get a nasty burn on my arm from a faulty toaster oven in our budget-priced kitchenette, and I spend my last day in paradise cutting off tips of giant aloe spikes from the hotel garden and squeezing the gummy juice on my oozing wound.

When we return, we find that the kennel has been frantically trying to call us at the cell number we left, but since we didn't have an international calling plan they couldn't get through. Barney has been very ill. Severe gastroenteritis, the receptionist says. We are presented with a bill for several hundred dollars of veterinary care along with our much-improved dog. But as Curt walks Barney to the car, he notices him limping in an odd manner, lifting his back left foot out as he walks and kicking it slightly to the side. At one point, he almost trips but regains his balance.

We take him back to the kennel where the manager claims no one noticed a problem with his leg. She follows us outside to take a look. "We sure didn't see that," she says, before walking back into the warm lobby. The three of us get in the car—sprained, burned, and limping. It is still February. And still cold.

Several days later, I walk behind Barney in the park and observe his back left foot moving in the odd limp-and-lift manner we saw at the kennel. His limp is less pronounced, but still visible. Although he seems okay with it,

I'm beside myself with worry. I'm certain that something happened while he was being boarded and become obsessed with finding out what it was.

I take him to our vet's clinic, where a kind woman doctor looks him over. His regular vet is on vacation, so she arranges for X-rays, explaining that he will have to be sedated. (Dogs, unlike people, cannot be relied upon to play dead for no good reason.) When the films are developed, she sees problems in his hip area and refers us to a surgeon. It takes ten days to get a consultation appointment, and I'm told not to feed Barney beforehand.

When we get to the surgery center, they have us wait in an examining room with nothing in it but a steel table and one chair. We wait for what seems like half an hour before a ponytailed man in his late thirties breezes into the sparse examining room with a younger man following behind. The surgeon pops Barney's X-ray into a light box on the wall and points to the ghost-like image of a round bone shaded with black.

"You see this," he says. "It's the hip socket." Then he points to a bone right under the socket. "This is his leg bone. It's totally luxated."

"What does that mean?" I ask.

"Not even in the socket anymore."

I stare at the picture of my dog's bones. Like all X-rays, it's cloudy in places, dark in others, and hard to make out clearly. But even I can tell the leg bone is missing its mark. And there's more. The doctor says his right hip is arthritic. That's what the pitted black spots are.

The doctor squats on the floor, lowering himself to Barney-height, and runs his hands over Barney's bones while the younger man watches and says nothing. When the doctor is done with Barney, he remains on the floor, and leans against the wall, folding his hands in his lap. He says there are three options for my dog: the first is a full hip replacement, which is very expensive and involves lengthy healing time. The second recommendation is a partial hip replacement—on just the left side. He explains this is a less complicated and less costly procedure that he believes would work well. "Of course," he says, "with Barney's age there are still the risks of surviving surgery, but the partial would have half the recovery complications and could make him much more comfortable."

"How much for the partial?" I've cut back to part-time hours since October in order to keep up with my schoolwork, and I'm keenly aware that my salary is half of what it used to be. He leans back against the wall and hugs his knees.

"About $3,500."

The look on my face must say it all. "There is another option," he says. "I can do nothing at all and his hip will continue to deteriorate. With that arthritis on the right hip, you may have some *real* problems soon."

If I choose surgery, he suggests, I should set something up soon, because his availability is tight right now. He'll have to check his schedule but he *thinks* he can squeeze me in at the end of March.

I don't mind the squatting. I'm more than fine with the ponytail. But for some reason, I get the feeling the other doctor is here specifically for *this* part of the examination—to watch the sales pitch, the closing techniques, like I'm buying a car or a big-screen television. Maybe this is how it is in the veterinary surgical world, but I feel rushed and confused and certainly not able to make a decision now.

"I'll have to think about it."

That evening, I watch Barney limp his way down the park road. Why did I wait so long to bring him to the park, to bring real joy to his life? Twelve years old and only two of them spent taking decent walks. As I study his face, so obviously happy to be here despite any pain he might have, I'm ashamed of myself and sharply aware of the lost time. An old childhoods song drifts into my head: *The leg bone connected to the hip bone. . . .*

His leg bone dips wildly before me. Not even connected to the hip bone, the doctor said. If Barney loses his ability to walk, he'll lose everything. I can't let that happen.

Two days later I call and make an appointment for a partial hip replacement. I force myself not to think about the money—I'll put it on a charge card, find a way to make it happen. By now, the doctor's schedule is full, I'm told. They schedule the operation for the first week in April.

CHAPTER 14

SPRING 2003

Usually when I return from a trip, I'm met by a wriggling mass of panting, whining *Ohjoyohjoyohjoyyou'rehome* dog. But instead, I'm greeted by my mother, who has been watching Barney while I was gone. She sighs with relief that her firstborn has made it home in one piece after traveling to Florida for a work-related conference. "Really, to go that far," she says. "A woman alone."

"I'm fine," I say, turning my head in an effort to divert her Revlon "Really Red" lipstick kisses from tattooing my cheek. "Where's Barney?"

Barney is at the back door, barely able to contain himself, wiggling and wagging, as he probably has been for the last three minutes. I open the door and bend down to his level, letting his happiness overtake me, welcoming the wet dog kisses on my face.

When Barney calms down, my mother and I sit at the kitchen table where I tell her all about St. Petersburg: the warm weather, the food, the hotel room. What I don't tell her is that after the conference I rented a car and took a side trip to Gibsonton, the winter home of a large number of circus and carnival sideshow performers to do research for a possible article.

On the way, I got lost in the pouring rain on I-75, traveling forty miles beyond the exit before turning around, only to find a depressing little hamlet of twenty-four hour bars and run-down trailers. I don't tell her how I sat in a booth in a tin-can diner adjacent to the Giant's camp (a trailer park owned by Al "The Giant" Tomaini and his wife, Jeanie "The Half Girl") eating a towering piece of spice cake across the aisle from a sullen, chain-smoking midget. She wouldn't understand.

Every time I take a trip without my husband, my mother tells me to make sure I don't look "too good." Her philosophy is that a tight skirt or a pretty dress makes a woman more of a target. Although the feminist in me rebels against the message, I hear her words each time I pack for a trip, remembering that on the night of the attack, I wore jeans with holes in the knees and an old checked shirt. *See?* I tell myself. *Proof that it doesn't matter what you wear.* But I'm not sure I believe that anymore. I temper my clothing choices when traveling. I don't look "too good." Not in the streets. Not in the airport. Not till I'm in the hotel or conference site or wherever it is I'm going.

As we talk, Barney lies at my feet under the table. I reach down and absentmindedly run my hands over his back. My fingers touch something wet and sticky. I draw my hand back and see my fingertips covered with a watery red substance. *Blood.*

What the . . . ? "What's wrong with Barney?"

My mother reacts defensively, as if I've hit her with a mop. "Nothing."

Glancing at the calm, happy head under the table, I don't see anything out of the ordinary. Then I notice a patch of dark, matted fur in the center of Barney's back. As I part the spot with my fingers, his skin peels off like an orange rind, complete with intact dog fur, exposing a shiny bed of red and white corpuscles. I scream.

When we get to the vet's office, all the vet can say is that it's a pretty bad scrape. "Looks like he tried getting under a fence. Maybe running after a squirrel or something."

Barney has never tried escaping under a fence. In fact, this dog amazes me with his blissful domesticity. He never seems to want to run off, not even on the rare occasions that present themselves—like when my husband leaves both the door to the garage and the garage door wide open—Barney just stands there, hovering around me, waiting for my cue.

Then I remember the deep grooves imprinted into the wide boards of the deck last winter when he attempted to claw his way to a critter taking shelter underneath. My mind scans the circumference of the deck, stopping at the gap between the ground and the boards, a space large enough for a rabbit or chipmunk to squeeze under, small enough for a big dog to get caught in. When I mention the gap to the doctor he says it's a good bet that something like that happened. "You just never know. That's the problem. They can't tell us."

The vet peels the fur back and throws the clot of hair and skin into the trash before writing a prescription for a round of antibiotics. When he reaches for a dog biscuit, Barney jumps up and dances in mid-air, his face conveniently level to the vet's hand. "Mind your manners, mister," I tell him. Then I remind the doctor about Barney's operation next week, asking if the antibiotics will affect the surgery.

"Hip surgery? *This* dog?"

Apparently he hasn't read the notes from the vet who examined Barney in February. I explain the limping after the kennel visit, the X-rays, the surgeon's diagnosis, and surgery date set for next week. He shakes his head.

"Any dog that can jump up for cookies like he did is not a candidate for hip surgery."

The doctor re-examines the X-rays and discusses Barney's options. In the end, I cancel the surgery (feeling triumphant over the ponytailed doctor and his hard sell). I schedule a date with him for teeth cleaning and the removal of a benign growth on the back of Barney's neck (two chores that were to be done while he was under anesthesia for the hip surgery), aware that my motivation for booking these services is, in part, generated by my gratefulness to this vet for getting us off the hook.

While Barney seems to be getting better, I'm getting worse. Ever since returning from Tobago, my bowels have been plagued by a serious bout of inertia. I'm vaguely nauseated all the time, constipated almost daily, and aware that something is very wrong with me. My acupuncturist recoils when he looks at my tongue. "Something is definitely off."

When I tell a friend who travels to Trinidad and Tobago frequently that I haven't felt well since my trip, she confides that the last time she went to Tobago she came home with intestinal parasites. That's when I remember the smoothie stand in the rainforest.

I was careful to drink only bottled water on the island. But when our sightseeing guide stopped at a roadside smoothie stand, I threw all caution to the wind, mostly to avoid being seen as a typical tourist. While my drink swirled around in the blender, I stood under a lush canopy of trees and watched a man wash his car in a stream behind the makeshift stand, not even thinking about where the smoothie maker got his water. When my drink arrived, I downed the super-sized concoction of unwashed blended fruit and water with gusto. Not a smart move.

My intestinal health becomes an obsession. I'm certain I have bugs in my system. Curt complains of many of the same symptoms, which only braces my theory until his clear up within a few weeks. Mine continue, no matter what I eat.

My doctor orders a test for intestinal parasites, which comes back negative. I find out from the acupuncturist that very few labs in this country are set up to test accurately for parasites because the condition is so rare in the States. Frustrated, I travel to Baltimore to the Johns Hopkins Travel Center clinic, where they tell me I should have come to them before the trip, not after. Yes, they say, you should peel all fruits and vegetables or boil them when traveling in the tropics. Yes, it is more than unwise to drink unfiltered water. The doctor takes blood, but sends the tests to the same lab as before since it's the only one my insurance will pay for. The results are the same. Negative.

I begin a food diary, furtively writing down every little thing I eat and the digested results of these meals. It reminds me of the expense diary I used to keep when I was in a Debtors Anonymous group, every penny accounted for—waste not, want not—although this is mostly waste *not*. Meanwhile, my writing is just as constipated, a struggle for words, each paragraph, each page a tortured accomplishment.

I have finished the essay on my father. Now I'm supposed to begin work on my thesis, the 150-page manuscript required for graduation, which will be about the time I spent as a singer in a new wave band in the 1980s. I write about the evolution of my hair: from brunette to eggplant to pink to fried blonde tresses as brittle as copper wire. I write about the high heels I wore onstage and how they were like little hills that kept me off balance, and about the audience of punk poseurs who sustained themselves on a steady diet of sarcasm and testosterone. I try to sing on the page, but I'm as self-conscious about the writing now as I was about the singing then. Each word is a small cut, a slice into the skin bleeding the truth of what I could not see then: Neglect. Self-destruction. An unfathomable longing to be heard. This is a story that does not have a good ending. The telling of it does not come easily.

On the way to the park, I hear a report on the radio about a guy who went over an embankment during a freak snowstorm out West and stayed alive for three days by melting snow and eating leftover taco sauce from foil packets. Maybe making a mess of things is not always so bad. Bad hips, bad guts, bad decisions. You use what you can to sustain yourself, to keep going, even if the going is slow.

By May, I'm still dragging. On most of my days off work, I end up drinking coffee and reading the paper until noon, then spending the rest of the afternoon grocery shopping or running nonessential errands in order to avoid the computer. But on a gray morning in mid-May, with only twenty-two pages written out of the fifty due to my professor by the end of the month, reality begins to kick in. Getting up from the table, I leave the kitchen and wander through the den, the foyer, the stairwell (three steps to the landing and ten to the upstairs hall) and into the guest room at the top of the stairs. Barney makes his way slowly behind me, laboring up the steps before settling on the floor near the bed where I sit, contemplating my next move.

The idea is to do some reading so I'll be inspired to write a couple of pages about the band years. But I'm tired as usual and, even worse, clouded by a fog of inertia. If I were serious about writing, I'd be in the room next door firing up the computer. Instead, I'm in the room that contains the guest bed, the one I gravitate to when I'm avoiding something. This is the land of procrastination and I know it. I'm sabotaging myself by walking into this space—willingly, willfully, regrettably.

Barney sprawls on the carpet in his "flatula" position (legs and arms splayed out, body spread like a dog pancake on the floor), his nose fixed like a compass point in my direction. This is his life's work, the masterful navigation technique my husband calls "the arrow." If anyone wants to find me, all they have to do is look for Barney and follow the direction his head is pointing. It never fails.

I get up from the bed and turn to the dresser that serves as a nightstand. Barney lifts his body off the floor and repositions, resetting his course so that the nose aims straight for me. I can feel his presence at my back, anchoring, grounding me. *You are here. You are here,* his body seems to say, and who am I to question such constancy? In the line of this compass I feel less like a drifting cloud and more like a fixed star in a black and brilliant sky—even if I'm slacking off, which I am.

As if in a trance, I open the top drawer of the faux-Chinese chest. The first thing that catches my eye is a small white cardboard box, one of many tiny department store jewelry boxes crammed in this hold. Inside the box are silver heart earrings with skull and crossbones cutouts and a black leather bracelet adorned with metal studs, remnants of my band days. I open a purple box adorned with the silver logo of a store that no longer exists. Hidden under a soft carpet of white cotton are two broken pieces of a silver bracelet, a gift given to me many years ago by the lead singer in a rock band I interviewed in my early journalism days. I place the bracelet back in its box and continue digging around in the pile of memories assembled over the years. A small, velvet bag holds three tarnished coins imprinted with Chinese characters—my old *I Ching* coins. I shake the coins out of the bag and press them in my palms, welcoming the cool smoothness against my skin.

Underneath all this junk is a large, full-color souvenir brochure from a 1969 Monkees concert. The Monkees get me going, setting off a panicked poking around the bottom of the drawer in search of my beloved 3-D Monkees ring (which I know is in here somewhere), but before I can find it, my fingers rest on the round, wooden beads of a rosewood and string necklace—my old mala.

I lay the mala on the dresser. Three long strands flow from one end of the circle string of beads, representing a human head and arms. On the other end are two similar pieces, representing legs. Using my fingers, I coax the necklace into its proper shape—the head and arms on top, the long round necklace body in the middle, the two legs on the bottom. I'm surprised at how faded the small, felt pompoms on the tip of each strand have become, each velvety point scuffed with the dirt of age. I gather the beads in my hand, studying the places where the deep rosewood stain has been rubbed to a golden umber. Involuntarily, my thumb begins moving up and down a section of bead as words form on my lips: *Nam-myoho-renge-kyo.*

These were the beads I brought to California for Nichiren Shoshu chanting. When not used for chanting, I looped the mala through my jeans as a kind of hip fashion accessory. I wore them everywhere—to parties, to job interviews, to band practice. They dangled from my waist the night of the attack. That was the last time I ever wore them.

The following day, I retrieve the bead mala from the guest room dresser and wrap it around a belt loop on my jeans, taking care to arrange it so that the three strands symbolizing the head and arms are in the correct position. It has been raining all day, and Barney and I have been waiting for a break in the weather. When the rain moves out, we immediately head for the park under gray but clearing skies. As we walk down the road, the mala hangs at my side and I feel like that young girl I used to be, swinging her hips through the streets of Berkeley as a song floats through an open window about a white bird in a golden cage.

Not long after the rape, I sat in a room filled with plants and paisley bedspreads and listened as West Coast feminists made me the center of their consciousness raising group. What happened to me was a terrible thing. But I had to understand that it was a political act, not a personal one. Rape was not a sexual crime, they explained. It was an act of power, rage, and politics. Someone quoted from a section of Eldridge Cleaver's *Soul on Ice* where he advocated raping white women as "a principle of black rebellion." This was not new, they pointed out, and certainly not the sole dominion of Cleaver and his political agenda. Raping women was a tactic used throughout history to intimidate and dominate entire communities.

Get over it seemed to be the underlying message, even though no one said those words. I needed to move on and get to work. We were at war, and I had to think of myself as a soldier in the battle for women's rights. Screw sexism. Stand up for your sisters. Don't take it personally.

I bought into it. And why not? It was better than feeling like shit. *Nothing personal,* I told myself. *Nothing to get hung up on.* Over the next few weeks I looked for jobs and sang at open mike gigs, playing my guitar and writing new songs. I tried to be a woman warrior, slamming guys who made disparaging remarks about women. But no matter how fiercely I argued with chauvinist pigs or how loudly I sang, I couldn't escape the hollow, ringing sound of the empty space that used to be me.

The park is fresh and green, the same color of those leafy asparagus ferns that hung from macramé plant holders in the room where nothing was personal. I caress the wooden beads of the mala hanging from my jeans and turn onto the Shark Trail, keeping to the pavement because the rain has made mud of everything else. From somewhere beyond the trees, an awful, strangled sound emerges. I freeze in my tracks. The sound becomes louder. At first, I think it's a woman screaming. (It's always a woman screaming that I hear when certain sounds echo in the air.) But no. It's lower, bassier, more nasal, like a duck in crisis mode. The chicks should be hatching by now. Perhaps hawks have swooped down and are carrying the babies away in their beaks.

Barney calmly tilts his head toward the sound and moves in its direction. As we continue down the dark, tree-covered trail, a gurgling, strangling noise surrounds me. I feel like I'm descending into hell.

We pass the swamp bog. I can't see anything—it's all noise here, frenetic, bassy. I want to turn back when suddenly the sound becomes recognizable. What I'm hearing are bullfrogs, hundreds of them, belching, bleating, squonking. As Barney and I stand there listening to the sound rise and fall, my fear turns to joy, that combination of delight and admiration I always feel when I hear frogs singing. There is something wondrous and noble about those who can live in the mud and still make beautiful music.

I find myself fingering the mala as I stare into the frog pond. After I left Berkeley, the chanting stopped, but the search for a spiritual connection did not. I continued to meditate and look for answers. I read and re-read Zen Mind, Beginner's Mind, a helpful book for a person who needed to start over again. I'd sit on my porch in the afternoons, breathing in, breathing out, trying to bring myself back to the present moment, even if only for seconds at a time.

The arrow is pointing forward. Barney's had enough of the frogs and their throaty chorus. He pulls the leash out to its full length and looks back at me, obviously saying "Let's move on," but I'm not quite ready. I stare at the dark waters, still sorting through memories. I don't want to let go of the frogs. Or the mala. Or the girl I used to be. But I have to. It's time.

"Coming, Master," I say to Barney as I follow him down the Shark Trail. Raindrops filter through the trees and land on my face where they flow like tears. I stick my tongue out to taste them. No salt. No bitterness. Just the clean, fresh newness of rain as it falls.

CHAPTER 15

SUMMER 2003

I'M SITTING IN A DARKENED ROOM RESISTING THE URGE TO BLINK while a blinding beam of light is aimed directly into my pupil.

"Yep. Just what I thought," the ophthalmologist says. "Floaters."

Looking past the chart glowing on the wall, I see my life go downhill before my eyes. *Floaters. Isn't that what old people have?*

"It happens with age," the doctor says. "What you're seeing is dried-up gel from the eye's viscous fluid. Your eyes will get used to it. Eventually you won't even see them anymore."

The first time I noticed the spots I thought I was seeing things. Barney and I were walking in the park. It was so hot that afternoon that waves of heat shimmered off the asphalt. I bent down and touched the pavement with my palm, trying to gauge how it must feel against a naked paw. *Hot. Blistering hot.* I wondered how Barney could stand it. As I stood up, a small black speck lazily floated past my field of vision. Instinctively, my head jerked back as my eyes searched out the offending insect. Before I could find it, another speck appeared, floating in that same slow freefall, this one more of a brownish-gray than black and shaped like a miniature cigar, before disappearing. Then I looked up to the sky and saw it again. It followed me as my head turned to the right. Floated by when I looked to the left. It began to dawn on me that this was not a bug, not dust, not even a bit of leaf or grass flying on the breeze.

The doctor clicks the flashlight off. His chipper voice drones on and on about other eye-related business, but I can feel my stomach sinking into doom territory, the place I immediately go when confronting physical changes of any kind. First the contacts had to go because of dry eyes. Now my eyeballs are literally desiccating in their sockets. It's the beginning of the end. I'm certain of it.

But within a few days, the ghosts floating across my field of vision begin to fade, reducing their annoying presence to an occasional gray blur. If I see them at all, it's usually when I'm walking with Barney, their presence indicated by shadowy specks drifting across a blank expanse of blue sky. As we walk and my eyes fill with the beauty of dappled sunlight bouncing off ever-changing shades of green, I lose my dismay over the floaters and start to think of them as markers of wisdom rather than age: I *am* seeing things I've never seen before. The veil between me and the world is lifting in small but significant ways. So what if pieces of it break off and dance in my eyes?

Some things I don't want to see. Barney is turning into an old dog before my eyes, his muzzle getting grayer, his hip knocking audibly as we walk through the stillness of summer afternoons. I tell the vet about it, a sound I can only describe as the grinding of bone against bone in an out-of-kilter socket.

"That's exactly it," he says cheerily, as if I'm a student of veterinarian forensics. Some dogs feel less pain than others, he tells me. "Barney's a Lab-Rottweiler. The combination makes him extremely pain-tolerant. Now if he was an Afghan . . . "

Maybe I'm an Afghan. I bruise easily and can't seem to shake whatever it is that is messing with my innards. Although the test results for the parasites come back normal, my doctor agrees to put me on a course of Flagyl, which eventually makes me break out in hives. Barney may not feel much pain from his hip, but the patches from April—the spot from the bad scrape and the area where the vet shaved him to remove a cyst—are still bald. At least three times a day, I run my fingers against the small bed of black bristles poking out from the skin, hoping to feel some softness, some semblance of fur growing back, but it always feels the same—short and bristly, and exactly like it was a week or two after being worked on.

I'm told not to worry, by both my doctor and Barney's vet. Barney needs more time. And it can take months for my system to return to normal after the bacterial bulldozing effects of the Flagyl. People passing give us curious looks, as if Barney is a refugee from an animal testing lab. My husband renames him Patches. A homeless guy hanging out in the park gazebo says "That dog looks just like I feel." Usually, when asked what happened, I just mutter something about surgery. What bothers me is that the patches are not the result of surgery, but just a scrape and the removal of a simple cyst.

By August, I feel better than I have in months, and I'm convinced I'm on the mend. But back in school for a second on-campus residency, it's obvious that my writing is still constipated. I start and I stop, skim the surface of the material I'm working with. All I want to do is let go of what I'm holding inside, but narrating the past while it still lives inside you is not an easy thing to do. To coax out the memories, I return to the park again and again, because it's here, where my thoughts unwind like the road before me, that I can start to make sense of what has happened and why. "The surface of the earth is soft and impressible by the feet of men," Thoreau said, "and so with the paths which the mind travels."

I walk and see my life as a child. I walk and see myself as a hopeful young woman starting out in the world. I walk and see how the singer in me lost all the songs inside her. I walk and I *see*.

August becomes September. Barney is beginning to relax more in the presence of other dogs walking in our vicinity, and I am too. We both are starting to trust the distance between us and whatever is coming down the road. With fall on the horizon, I'm surprised to be singing the praises of September. How could I have missed this before? The skies sparkling like a freshly cleaned window, the sun soft as flannel, the air so sweet and delicious; it's like breathing in clarity itself.

On one of those brilliant September afternoons, Barney pulls me toward a stream near the road where, earlier in the spring, raccoon traps had been set with oily bait. He sniffs around the area, eyes dancing with excitement, no doubt hot on the trail of some small, pitiful creature or searching for a minute particle of raccoon bait still scenting the grass. I let the leash uncoil full-length, watching him dash back and forth below the concrete viaduct that diverts the stream under the road. Although there are probably mosquitoes lurking, I move closer to the dark waters to examine the lace of bubbly scum etching the surface, and as I do, a dream entry from an old journal comes to mind, one of hundreds of pages I've been going through as research for my thesis.

In the dream, I'm walking down a dark alley toward a stage door. The door opens, and, just as I'm about to walk in, I hear a terrified voice coming from somewhere in the alley—a girl calling me by name, begging for help. I look in the direction of the voice but see only darkness. And then there is silence. In that black void, I know something terrible is happening. But instead of helping the girl, I turn my back, step through the stage door, and close it behind me.

The pond sharpens into focus again, the glass surface acting like a scrying mirror revealing the dark underside of the past. How could I have not seen it then? Even now, sitting in the audience twenty years later, the abandonment is almost too painful to watch. This was my last chance after my aborted attempt in California. I sacrificed myself on the altar of desire—to perform, to be loved and adored, to be anyone else other than that wounded girl. In those days, I wrapped myself in the tough girl persona; it was all *fuck you* and *fuck that* as I strutted across the stage among screaming guitars and crashing drums, stomping an imaginary lover under my six-inch heels while I wailed "These boots are made for walking."

I've been writing about those boots (metallic blue, plastic, real toe-crushers) and the seedy clubs where the smell of beer and Freon and old vomit hit you when you loaded in during the day. I write about some of the crazy people I played with, men like my LSD-tripping guitar player who had a hair-trigger temper and a juvenile rap sheet, the David Bowie wannabe bass player (who sold mobile homes during the day and rifled through my wallet at night), and my wacked-out drummer—a long-haired rocker I adored even though his behavior often bordered on the sociopathic.

My professor advises me that you can't write until you have enough distance from it. But twenty years has to be more than enough distance. So I take a short trip to Cincinnati to revisit the scene of the crime. Then I get down to work, dredging memories of dead-end gigs, record company hacks, and twenty-something men on a ceaseless journey to be famous and get laid, changing the names to protect the guilty. I start and stop and then begin all over again:

Being the only woman in a rock band is like living in a locker room. The only thing the guys talk about is women, girls, cunnies, honnies, 'tang, and tits.

And music.

Sometimes.

My band and I are talking about music. About Pat Benatar's band, who we're not supposed to like because they're too "commercial." But Johnny, our guitar player, says Neil Giraldo is killer. And Pat, well, what can you say? We're debating whether to take up a last-minute offer of free tickets and backstage passes for the show at Riverfront Coliseum. For once, we reach a consensus quickly. We cut rehearsal short, get in the van, and go.

Stix, my drummer, calls me "Little Pat." Like her, I'm tiny and a soprano and wear spandex pants. He's hoping I'll become famous like her and catapult him to the big time. From my fourth row seat in the darkened Coliseum, I watch Benatar onstage, awed by the power of her voice. I look around at the thousands of people and imagine being in front of them. Just the thought of it terrifies me.

Backstage, the boys talk with Pat's band as if they're old friends. Stix says the drummer tightens his heads the same way he does. My guitar player and Neil Giraldo both like to use extra reverb on their effects. Pat never appears, but her road manager tells me she uses a Shure SM58 microphone, just like mine. One big happy family. Except they're hot shit and we're nothing.

I hang around the hospitality table, nibbling at cheeses, ham, some kind of dip with artichokes in it. They've got a bunch of stuff in a big tortilla shell that Johnny says is a taco salad. He knows because he's seen it on the menu at Chi-Chi's in Tri-County. I plop a scoop onto my paper plate where the mysterious ingredients are revealed: lettuce, a layer of beans, a layer of meat, shredded cheese, with a dab of sour cream and browning guacamole on top. Apparently it's some kind of new California thing.

Out in the parking lot, we're all high from hobnobbing with rock royalty. A cool breeze blows off the river and for the moment, anything seems possible. Stix puts his arm around me and gives me a squeeze. His eyes have that troll doll sparkle to them and I know something is up.

We walk on for a few beats in silence before he pulls his arm away and looks out over the tarmac stretching before us.

"So what d'ya think?" I ask.

Stix tosses his blonde hair over his shoulder and smiles down at me.

"I'm thinking of that taco salad."

"Yeah?"

"Hope you didn't eat it."

"Why?"

"'Cause I peed in it."

I have plenty of material like this. Outrageous stuff, funny as well as just plain strange. But that's part of the problem. What I'm writing is a series of scenes, not a story. What doesn't make it to the page are all the things I still haven't reconciled, the deeper threads that could only be pulled apart with more distance. So when I write about opening for one of my favorite punk bands, I detail the excitement of being backstage with them and the crush of the punks in the mosh pit, but say nothing about how my own voice terrified me.

It was a sold-out show. Bogart's was filled to the rafters—all twelve hundred seats as well as the aisles and bar. I was thrilled to be on the bill with X and their lead singer Exene, a poet and songwriter I idolized. As usual, we didn't get a stage check; the lead act took up all the time. So it was a surprise when we got on stage and the monitors were working. For once, I could hear myself—*really* hear myself. As my voice thundered through the massive PA system, it became a force of its own, powerful, undeniable and, for some reason, so frightening that it sucked the breath out of me. For the rest of the set I sang off-key, cowering before the speakers, knowing the singer I could be was the one I was afraid of.

This was the story of the girl in the alley, but somehow she never makes an appearance in my manuscript. Even the alley itself is left out, that very real, very scary no-man's land I crossed into in the early morning hours after each show was over.

The deserted streets and back alleys of all the bars and clubs I ever played all blur together as one dark and terrifying place. But one always stands out—the Alley Cat, a gay bar that hosted punk and new wave music in an attempt to drum up business during the week. The club was literally located in an alley, a narrow, cobblestone corridor hidden in the heart of downtown Cincinnati. At 2 a.m., after all the cords were unplugged and the cables were wrapped and the instruments rested in their cases, it was time to load the equipment into the van—no excuses made for a ninety-five pound girl singer. My body tightened in fear as I walked alone into that alley lugging a forty-pound Farfisa keyboard. The van was only a few yards away but it felt like miles. Passing an overflowing dumpster, I'd hold my breath until I knew for sure no one was hiding behind it. Sometimes, I'd carry on whole conversations with an imaginary band mate so that whoever might be hiding in the shadows would think someone was behind me.

"Yeah, I got it," I'd say. "Be right there. Okay, okay. Inna minute."

After dumping the equipment in the van, I'd quickly make my way back into the club where I was "safe." Although with these guys, "safe" was a relative term.

When they peed in salads or talked about the ugly chick that gave good head or indulged in rounds of jokes about the pretty blonde who was kidnapped in a mall parking lot and later found raped and dead in a deserted barn, I never said a word. I just sang what I was supposed to sing, laughed at their stupid jokes, walked onto that stage, and shut the door behind me. Though the dream showed me exactly what I was doing, I ignored it at the time. I left the part of me who hurt out there in the dark so I wouldn't have to face her pain.

Now, the denial I've clung to for so long is rising to the surface. No wonder I've preferred the haze of summer to the clarity of fall. Bit by bit, pieces of time are drifting toward me, like lacey scum floating on top of a pond. *Here it is. And here.* What was once invisible is right in front of my face. Whether I write it or not, I'm beginning to see it clearly. This time, there is no turning away.

CHAPTER 16

FALL 2003

LYING IN BED, I STARE AT THE CEILING AND LISTEN TO THE STEADY bellows of Barney's panting. This is the third time he's woken me tonight. "Shut up!" I yell into the dark. The sound stops for a moment in reaction to my voice. Then it begins again followed by a noxious cloud of dog fart. "Jesus, Barney." I grab the sheets and turn in the opposite direction of the dog bed. Barney gets up and repositions himself on the cedar-filled cushion. He drops down with an audible sigh before the sound starts up again.

Barney pants at night. He pants during the day. He pants when we walk now, even though cooler weather has set in. I've begun to call him "Panty Boy," a name he seems pleased with, but then again, he rarely seems displeased. My sister once said Barney must be stupid because he seems so happy all the time. Her boyfriend shot back, "So you think if someone is happy, they're stupid?" It was a good question.

Like most dogs, when Barney pants, he looks especially happy (mouth open, turning up slightly up at the corners in a doggie grin). And he pants a *lot*. It's late October but still hot out, so I chalk it up to the weather— although the sheer volume of the panting does seem a bit excessive. And then there's the other problem: even though it's been over six months since the scrape and the cyst on his back were removed, his hair still hasn't grown back. It just doesn't seem right, so I bundle him into the car and travel more than an hour to western Maryland to see Dr. Kummel, his canine dermatologist. The doctor, as usual, is efficient and coolly fashionable in black slacks and a sophisticated designer blouse. Barney seems happy to see her until it's time for the examination. It takes three assistants and a muzzle to get him up on the examining table.

She asks about his health. I tell her about his hair loss and mention the panting as an aside. She asks if he's been unusually thirsty lately, and I have to admit, he does drink a lot of water. How about his appetite? Has he seemed exceptionally hungry lately? I laugh. "He's always hungry." I mention his increasing flatulence as a joke, but she's not laughing.

"I want to rule out the obvious," she says. She takes a razor blade and scrapes some skin off each of the two patches on his back. Twenty minutes later, I hear her high heels clicking in the hall. The door opens, and she looks serious. "Sorry to tell you this, but he's got the classic signs of Cushing's disease."

There are times when the curtain falls away and suddenly you're left looking at your own denial. After the scare around Barney's hips, I protected myself by refusing to get anxious over his vulnerability. Along with the panting and loss of hair, I had noticed that he'd been drinking a lot of water—bowl after bowl—but I thought he was just thirsty. As far as being hungry—well, Barney was always hungry. And the slowness, lethargy, farting; that could all be attributed to old age—right? If love isn't blind, it at least encourages a lazy eye.

Dr. Kummel sends us back to our primary care vet, with instructions to have him administer a complete blood count test. Barney endures an eight-hour day of blood monitoring, and when I come to pick him up I'm told he has chronically elevated ACTH levels (which indicate Cushing's), but they have to do more testing to determine whether the disease is adrenal or pituitary-based. About 80 percent of the time, the vet tells me, the problem is with the pituitary glands and can be controlled with medication.

The next blood test takes half a day to administer. The results are not what I want to hear. Barney's problem clearly stems from an adrenal tumor.

I'm given a referral to the veterinary surgical center for removal of the tumor while Barney gets a prescription for a cortisone-based pain medication for his arthritis. There is nothing that can be done for the Cushing's save surgery.

I am not handling this well.

The following week, I attend a graduate program field trip to New York City to visit with publishers and editors. We hop from the editorial suites of national magazines to agents' offices to a major publishing house—a whirl-wind of glass offices overlooking the Manhattan skyline where a book-lined conference room smells of dust and leather. I have forgotten about Barney's troubles for the moment. While on a break, I sneak into Macy's and buy a long suede coat with faux-fur lining. As we sit and talk to an editor at the *New Yorker*, I drape the fur coat over my shoulders, imagining myself as a quirky, dramatic writer-star meeting with my editor. While our host shares magazine secrets, my skin begins to itch, and the itch spreads across my arms, back, wherever the coat touches me. For the rest of the meeting, I squirm and scratch, barely hearing what he says.

Back home, I stroke Barney's own troublesome fur coat, wondering how he feels under his skin. I make an appointment with a specialist who is frank about Barney's chances. First of all, he's an older dog. The surgery is com-plicated and invasive and there is always the chance at his age that he will not survive the operation. Apart from that, he doesn't know what they will find until they open him up. The tumor may be benign or cancerous. They may be able to remove all of it or they may not. There's every possibility the surgery will go well. There's every possibility it won't. He cannot guarantee anything except this: If I do not elect to do the surgery, Barney will die within six months.

At first I say nothing. Then I want to know how he would die. "Most likely internal bleeding," he says. He notes it's not that bad a way to go. In the background, as if almost in a dream, I hear him say, "His systems would shut down and it's like he'd go to sleep."

I walk out of the office dazed. We go straight from the vet to the park where we walk in silence. Barney is as happy as ever now that he's out on a walk and I'm grateful he has no way of understanding what the vet said. I watch him lumber slowly down the road, my heart breaking with every step.

I don't know what to do, whether to put him through the risk of surgery or to let nature take its course. I just don't know.

That night, I discuss the options with my husband. We're both at a loss. I go to bed early and listen to the measured panting of my precious Barn, thinking, *Goddamn fall. It's got me once again.*

The next day, while we're walking in the park, I mull over the surgery and decide the odds aren't good enough. I won't put Barney through it. As he vigorously sniffs a short holly bush, I vow that I'll make his last six months good ones, full of walks and hot dogs and lots of love. We cross over to the meadow where I make a list in my head: I'll cook him hamburger and rice and marrow bones and put his head in my lap and tell him he is my best friend, the best dog ever. I'll line his bed with flannel sheets and roll up another sheet to make him a little pillow. I'll take him with me everywhere.

A day or so after I notify the surgeon of my decision, I wake to the sound of an odd, hacking cough coming from somewhere near the foot of our bed. I get up and knock into Barney who is stumbling around the room. When I turn on the light, I can see dark red splotches dotting the white berber carpet. I press my finger to one of the spots and recognize the rusty smell. *Blood.* Barney coughs again, sneezing, and droplets of blood shower the carpet by his feet. Panic fills my chest. My dog is sneezing *blood.*

We take Barney into the kitchen where Curt makes use of his Boy Scout skills to dampen a towel as a compress for Barney's nose. On the way to the emergency veterinary hospital, Curt sits in the back holding the towel to Barney's nose while I keep saying, "It's okay, B. Don't worry. It's okay."

He doesn't seem half as worried as we are.

By the time we get him to the hospital, the bleeding has stopped. Ironically, the emergency vet hospital is located at the same surgery center I took him to for the consultation. The emergency crew runs a battery of tests that are inconclusive. Then they hand us a bill for hundreds of dollars and tell us to call the surgeon during office hours. When I do, he is baffled. The adrenal tumor normally does not cause nosebleeds.

But medication can. I look up information on the pain medication the vet prescribed for Barney's hips and find out that some dogs, especially seniors, can get nosebleeds while on nonsteroidal anti-inflammatory drugs. Barney has been on this medication for over two weeks now. Although it's only a guess, both his regular vet and the surgeon agree I should stop the medication right away.

A few days later, just before Thanksgiving, he has another brief nosebleed episode. And then another. When I sit down to talk with Barney's regular vet, I tell him I'm beginning to wonder if I should consider the surgery. He's blunt about the nosebleeds. "Before you do anything, you need to know what's going on. If he has nasal cancer, forget about the adrenal surgery."

Apparently the only facility in the entire region that has the equipment for canine magnetic resource imaging is in Virginia. It costs nearly $1,000 for the service. At first, I balk, but the need to know what's going on with him is too great. A week later, I drive Barney to the Iams Pet Imaging Center in Vienna, a state-of-the-art facility so advanced that I'm told hospitals sneak human patients in after-hours so they can use the technology. It's raining and keeps on raining, a day of tears coming from the sky, and that feels right to me. While they prepare Barney for his MRI, I go next door to a Taco Bell for lunch and slip on the wet tile near the door, barely averting an MRI of my own.

Slippery floors, rising waters, walking on ground that no longer feels able to hold you: this is how it feels facing the possibility of losing someone you love. Barney leaves the Iams Center still groggy and slumps gratefully in the backseat of the car. By the time we get to the Beltway, the rain has turned into a downpour. One truck after another passes, splashing torrents of water across my windshield. I lean forward, turn up the wipers, and keep my speed steady, even though I can barely see what's in front of me. "Don't worry Barn-o," I say to my sleeping dog, "We'll get home okay. You'll be fine, sweet boy. Just fine."

CHAPTER 17

MELTING

THREE DAYS INTO DECEMBER, I GET UP EARLY AND TAKE BARNEY TO the park. There's a chill in the air that hasn't been there before, and for the first time this season, I notice how bare the trees are, how completely the colors of fall have been replaced by the brown nakedness of bark and tangled undergrowth. In the space between the trees, I can see much further into the woods than before.

Clarity is my mission today. Yesterday, Barney's doctor called and said the MRI revealed no problems with his nasal passages. I should be glad, but it means we're back to where we were and I can't help thinking about how crazy it is that I spent $1,000 to find out that the nosebleeds, which stopped a few days after the tests, were most likely a reaction to the medication. Before hanging up the phone, the vet asks if I've made a decision about the surgery. The longer I wait, he reminds me, the more risky the operation will be. Just weeks ago I was certain I didn't want him to be operated on, but facing the immediate possibility of losing him changes everything. I tell him I'll let him know.

I'm grateful this is happening during winter break. Even though progress is slow, I've piled up quite a few pages on the band manuscript—enough that, for now, anyway, I don't have to worry about the writing, only Barney. For one whole day, I sit around in a kind of daze, not able to think about much of anything. Then I decide to sleep on it. When I wake, I still don't know what to do. So, after multiple cups of strong coffee, I do the only thing I do when I can't do anything else: pile Barney into the car and take him for a walk.

When we get to the park, it's empty except for a couple of battered-looking crows, who caw at us once or twice before poking sullenly at the hard ground. The meadow is covered with a blanket of hoar, tiny crystals that melt into dew at the touch of our steps. But at least the sun is out.

Gravitating toward the sun, I head for the embankment between the road and the Shark Trail where the frost has already burned off. As soon as we reach the grass, Barney starts inhaling the ground like it's a long, crazy line of canine cocaine. He runs up and down the median strip, snorting with pleasure, his whole body wriggling as his nose mows down the dried grass. I watch him sucking down scents with that big black ball of a nose that I have kissed so many times, and I can't help laughing. Suddenly, there is no doubt as to what I should do. This dog still loves life and I love him too much not to try and save him.

When we get home, I call the veterinary hospital and schedule the surgery.

Twenty-four hours before Barney's operation, large, wet, snowflakes swirl outside in the yard. It's the first snow of the season and, as usual for this time of year, the event is brief and benign, leaving a thin dusting of glittering white stuff on the ground and nothing on the roads. By afternoon, the temperature reaches forty-five degrees, and Barney and I head out to the park under sunny skies. As we pass his favorite winter walking grounds (a large field of stubby mown weeds and sea oats), he stops to investigate a clump of dried grass.

Looking at him, I'm overwhelmed by the desire to tell him what's going to happen tomorrow—to have a conversation like you would with a child about to get his tonsils removed. Barney lifts his leg, a big smile of satisfaction spreading across his face as he relieves himself. Perhaps its better he doesn't know. I've spent three-quarters of my life worrying about what will happen in the future, and three-quarters of that has never happened. Barney's lucky to be able to sniff a patch of ground the day before surgery and know only the sweet essence of that moment.

I try to let go of my thoughts and be as fully present as my dog, to enjoy the blue-sky day, my wiggly boy, the warmth of the sun, but I'm blunted by the burden of what I know: this may be the last time Barney and I walk together.

As we approach the gatehouse, snow melts in puddles all around us and we can't help but get our feet wet. A car passes us and the driver looks over. We are an odd pair, my dog and I—me in my beret and sunglasses, he with his bad hip and swaying gait—but at this point, I don't care what anyone thinks of us. When we reach the gatehouse, I turn to head back and notice two sets of wet footprints stamped into the gray asphalt of the park road—size five-and-a-half boots accompanied by wet doggie paws—the tracks left by Barney and me walking together. Within the hour, they will disappear as if they never existed.

Buddha says it is our inability to accept impermanence that causes suffering. Logically, I understand that everything is in transition, but seeing those soon-to-be-vanishing paw prints is almost too painful to bear. As we walk down the road, I struggle to hold back tears. Birds sing sweet songs in the unexpected warmth. The sun caresses my face and for a moment I forget about the surgery. It's a beautiful day, one full of the promise of spring even though we are hurtling toward the end of December. Suddenly, I see how much I contribute to my own suffering.

Whenever faced with bad news, I immediately brace myself for the worst. I lay down the white flag, accept defeat, keep myself safe by not even attempting to hope for the best. Walking down the road, I try to consider the possibility of Barney surviving this ordeal and am amazed at how hard it is for me to do. Merely willing myself to think this way feels like a Herculean task, as if the thought itself is an immovable boulder. A voice inside says keep going, lift this weight, admit the possibility of Barney being well, but I can't. In the midst of this struggle, it becomes clear to me how incredibly hard it is to stay hopeful, how strong you have to be to keep your heart open in the face of disappointment.

I never understood how much courage it takes to have hope.

All these years, I've always thought of myself as a realist, smugly superior to those hope-full, faith-full idiots because I knew what they didn't: that no matter what you do, awful things happen. Why even pretend otherwise?

On the way back to the car, I start evaluating this pessimism of mine. Thirty years have passed since the attack in California and thirty-four since my father died. It's been twenty years since the self-debasement of my foray into punk rock. In that time, good things have happened as well as bad. I reflect on this as Barney stops to sniff under a pine tree. A car passes us on the road. *What the hell do I know?* I'm not God or Buddha or the ultimate decider of anyone's fate. Who am *I* to say that good things can't happen?

Just before we reach the parking lot, I stop and bend down to kiss the scratchy square patch on Barney's back. "You never know," I say to him. We continue toward the car, and I realize the truth of that statement. This morning it snowed. Now it's almost fifty degrees, and I'm sweating in my ankle-length down coat. *You never do know, do you?* When spring returns, it's possible we could still be here—a sway-backed dog, a woman in a beret and sunglasses—walking toward the gatehouse, stepping through puddles, leaving our muddy footprints behind to bake in the sun.

CHAPTER 18

WINTER 2004

Barney parks himself on the bedroom floor and watches me as I pack item after item into a black suitcase. As usual whenever I pack, he's very quiet. He knows whenever I put things in the rolling black box it means I'm going away without him.

Before the nosebleeds, before the Cushing's, before the MRI and surgery date, my husband and I had booked a trip for the second week in December to Fort Lauderdale to see the annual Winterfest Boat Parade. Both Curt and I had been to the parade years ago, and we talked often of going back to see South Florida's mega-yachts gliding up and down the canal of the Intracoastal Waterway festooned with glittering lights and tableaus of corny holiday pageantry. A reasonable person would have canceled the trip or moved the surgery to a later date, but I convinced myself that scheduling the surgery during our trip was a way to make the best of a bad situation. Barney needed to spend three days in the hospital either way.

We all go to great lengths to avoid things we don't want to face. The truth was I couldn't bear the thought of sitting in a plastic chair flipping through copies of *Dog Fancy* knowing the doctor might come out of surgery and tell me Barney was gone. I didn't want to go home and walk through the house past his dog bowls and cedar bed and the big, black Kong toy that drove him delirious with delight. I was a coward who justified nonrefundable airfare as a legitimate excuse to leave her best friend alone in a hospital during major surgery.

On the morning of our departure, we load the bags and herd a happy dog into the car; he's sure this invitation to ride in the backseat means he's coming with us on our journey. At the veterinary hospital, I take him for a short walk in the grassy area next to the hospital parking lot and tell him everything will be fine. Then I bring him inside the hospital and hand him over to a young female vet tech, turning away before she leads him through the swinging doors of the surgery.

On the way to the airport, traffic ties up the interstate for thirty minutes, which makes us late for our flight. When we finally get through security, we have to run all the way down to the end of the terminal to make it to our gate on time. As soon as I get on the flight, my obsessive-compulsive relationship with germs goes into high alert. All through the flight I keep my gloves on and cover my face with Kleenex whenever I hear anyone coughing or sneezing. Unfortunately, the person coughing and sneezing the most on the plane is sitting right next to me. By the time we arrive at the Fort Lauderdale airport, my shins are so sore from the pre-flight jog that I can barely walk, and Curt's sniffles have turned into a full-blown cold.

We're not even out of the rental car garage before I'm sniping at Curt (*Dammit, use a Kleenex, not your hand!*). Our hotel is an exquisite little boutique property directly on the Intracoastal Waterway, but our charming room is the size of a walk-in closet and I'm already trying to figure out how to avoid touching anything Curt has touched. When I tell him not to handle anything on my side of the bed, he acts like it's a personal insult. I have a feeling this trip is not going to be quite the pleasant distraction I had anticipated.

Meanwhile, Barney is on my mind. While his surgery is underway, we take a water taxi tour of the lavish homes lining the canals with a captain at the helm who is channeling a bad comic. The green-blue waters of the Intracoastal shimmer in the sun as our boat of tourists bobs alongside mega-yachts and glossy speedboats with names like Fast Company and Suck My Wake. We slow down while passing a rambling white stucco faux-villa. The captain announces, "There's the house Lee Majors tried to sell after divorcing his wife. You try to sell a house without a Fawcett, ha ha."

The jokes keep coming as we pass the mansions of celebrities, rich people, and the business giants who dreamed up America's chain stores. Peering at these multimillion dollar compounds, I alternate between envy and revulsion (how many marble statues can you cram around an infinity pool?), the whole time stealing glances at my watch, keenly aware that while we're yukking it up with Captain Clever on the high seas, Barney is on an operating table.

Finally, I get a call on my cell phone from the doctor, who has just left surgery. Between the boat motor, the captain's jokey patter, and the bad signal, I can barely hear him, but I catch enough of what he's saying to know that Barney has survived the surgery and is in recovery. The doctor says the adrenal tumor has been successfully removed and starts to say something about his liver, but I can't understand. I keep saying "What? What?" He tells me to check back later.

"Barney's okay," I tell Curt. I'm so relieved that I put on the set of reindeer antler ears offered by the boat's first mate and have a picture taken with the captain. But later that night, when I call to check on Barney, a vet tech tells me his electrolytes are off, and she's going to have to tell the doctor. I ask how he's doing. "Well, he's an old dog," she says, "and he's just had surgery."

Now I'm getting my punishment. My dog needs me and I'm not there for him. I sit on the dock and watch the lights bounce on the water. I could beat myself up or drink margaritas until I'm oblivious, but I'm beginning to lose my taste for both self-flagellation and alcohol. Instead, I close my eyes and envision Barney in a crate in the back of the veterinary hospital. I imagine stroking his head, speaking to him as if I were there, telling him in soothing tones that everything will be okay. They say patients who are prayed for while in surgery do better than the average patient. I have no idea how you test that one, but it's worth a shot. As I send my love to him, a feeling of peace and comfort enters my body. There is some kind of healing going on here, but whether it is for him or me, I don't know.

The small hotel room gets smaller as Curt's cold gets worse. We talk our way into a larger one, but it still has only one bed, which makes avoidance difficult. Curt spends most of his time inside watching the television nonstop. I walk in at one point and see an unshaven, bewildered old man on the screen looking as sick as my husband. Saddam Hussein has just been captured. For some reason, it's hard to get excited about it.

Finally, I get to speak to the doctor again and I can hear every word. Despite the previous night's scare, Barney is recovering nicely. They took out the adrenal tumor, which turned out to be benign. But when they opened him up they found another tumor, a malignant one, on his liver. "We tried to remove as much as we could," he tells me. "But we couldn't get it all." He reassures me that liver tumors are slow-growing, but it's not the news I wanted. I had prepared myself for two options: Barney would either recover completely or not make it through. I didn't plan on things being almost-okay.

Curt's cold gets better and we spend our last evening in Florida watching the boat parade, a floating vision of holiday decorations, loud Christmas music, drunken Santas, and scantily clad female elves shouting *Ho ho ho!* from bobbing decks. By the time we get back to Maryland, Barney's feeling much better but I'm feeling worse, having picked up the bug Curt had in Florida.

At home, both Barney and I spend the majority of our time sleeping. A few days after the surgery, his back legs become unsteady. His doctor gives him a shot of Adequan, a painkiller, which seems to help, although he walks more slowly than before. Eventually my cold goes away, but not the tiredness that accompanied it. Nothing seems to have been resolved, not Barney's health, or my struggles writing about the band, or the chronic exhaustion that plagues me from time to time. Still, I make sure we get to the park, even if it's only for a short walk.

On the eve of the winter solstice, Barney and I stand in the meadow and watch the last amber hues of sunset wash over the treetops. It's 4:30 in the afternoon, and as soon as the sun disappears, dusk settles in for the night. From somewhere above, a crow calls out, his cry slicing through the chill air. In its wake is nothing but silence. The shortest day of the year has come. For three months now, the light has been waning and I can't help but think how Barney and I have been on the wane, too.

As the sky fills with twilight, I stand in the stillness and hold on to the realization that we are at a turning point. Even though the light appears to have retreated, the days will be growing longer from now on. Knowing this gives me strength to wait out the long nights ahead.

A week and a half later, on New Year's Day, I'm in the backyard with a pooper scooper in hand, mining for dog doo like a treasure hunter on the beach. Barney has mostly been confined to the yard for the past three weeks, and the obligations, so to speak, have been piling up. The odd thing is that I find the task strangely satisfying. *Out with the old, in with the new.* How often do you get the opportunity to wipe the slate clean as easily as this?

After a thorough sweep of the lawn, I begin checking in the garden beds. Under the branches of a great pine tree, I find a mound of small dark pellets resembling the scat of a raccoon or fox next to a cluster of semidigested red berries. Alarmed that Barney will get sick if he eats this stuff, I move in to pick it up and notice a smattering of black feathers in the pile as well as long quills of feather spine. I'm not sure what I'm looking at—a dead bird's entrails or the regurgitated remains of some predator's New Year's Eve feast. The animal in me wants to extend my senses to find the answers—to touch it, to sniff it, to sort through the remains like a gypsy sifting through tea leaves—but the human in me is repulsed. I force myself to lower the plastic bag to the ground and scoop up the seeds, scat, and feathers.

I am a somewhat superstitious woman, the product of a long line of female forbearers who have relied on fear-based habits and rituals to influence the future: my mother, who refuses to hand open safety pins to another person for fear something bad will happen; my aunt, wearer of a red "bendel," a piece of string on her wrist to ward off the evil eye; and my grandmother, their mother, who passed on all this from the "old country."

But it didn't stop there. In our suburban, middle-class New Jersey home, singing was not allowed before breakfast, because doing so meant something bad might happen at night. I couldn't talk about anything important on

Friday nights, because it might jinx the possible outcome. And whenever anyone mentioned something good that might happen, you had to knock on wood (or your head if no wood was around).

While resisting some of my family's more ridiculous traditions, I continue looking for signs, which to me means paying attention when the world speaks to me and hoping I get it right. Maybe it's just human, this need to know more than we can, to have some control over what, in the end, is not under our control at all. Poking at the remaining bird guts, seed, and scat with a loose stick, it's easy to understand why ancient Babylonians believed reading the still-warm livers and entrails of sacrificed animals could divine the future. So many twists and turns—the hidden revealed right before your eyes.

I don't have the luxury of pretending not to know Barney's future. The seers of veterinary science have read his liver and predicted his fate. "A slow-growing tumor," they say, although no one can tell me how slow.

Barney suns himself in the yard, watching as I move across the lawn scooping up his waste. By now he's gotten used to the myriad things I do that must make no sense to his dog mind (like stopping him from chasing squirrels, putting wonderful-smelling garbage in a closed container, sitting in the house when we could be outside walking and, of course, collecting poop—probably one of the few human habits that might actually seem like a good idea).

I set the bag down, sit next to him, and rub his cheek with my palm. His eyes narrow in doggie ecstasy as he leans his big head into my hand. This dog trusts me so completely that it makes me ashamed. I'm not sure I deserve it.

When Sundance fell ill and the vet told me there was nothing they could do, my world started spinning. Everything blurred at the edges. The only thing I could see with any clarity was my dog, sick; my dog, dying. I put him down the same day his chest X-ray showed his body riddled with cancer. This is what I cannot forgive myself for: that I fell apart and did not bring him home. That I didn't spend the night comforting him and telling him how much he meant to me. That I did not give him the choice, this dog that was so independent and fiercely free, to leave this world on his own.

I put my own suffering over his, and all I could think of was stopping my pain, the pain of knowing he was going to die.

People tell you that you're doing the right thing when you put a sick dog down, but for me it was the worst kind of betrayal. Sundance, this hero dog of mine, always hated the vet's office—shaking as soon as we walked in, constantly angling his way back toward the front door, whining to get out. "Look at you," I'd say to him, laughing. "You're such a coward."

What did I know? The vet's office was the only place, the only time I saw this dog exhibit fear. Maybe he could read the future much better than I.

After finishing up my poop-collecting duties, I sit beside Barney in a spot of sun on the lawn and stroke him softly, steeling myself against the urge to cry. Silently, I make a promise to him. This time, I won't screw up like I did before. This time, I swear, I'll do it right.

CHAPTER 19

TUESDAYS IN THE PARK

MARCH BEGINS THE WAY IT USUALLY DOES—COLD AND DAMP—BEFORE taking pity on the winter-worn with a sultry, sixty-degree day. Outside my window, green shoots push through the earth. Purple and white crocuses curl on their stems and long wands of bright yellow forsythia brazenly burst into bloom. Barney is blooming as well, showing no signs of a failing liver and every indication that he plans on sticking around for a while.

After hacking away at the band manuscript for most of the morning, I decide to take a break. Bundling Barney in the car, I drive to the strip mall across from the park, find a parking space, and walk Barney across the street past a closed gate announcing "Park closed on Tuesdays."

I know the park isn't open on Tuesdays. But ever since we've been coming here, joggers, bikers, walkers, all kinds of people go right around the closed gate as if it's just another day. Apparently, there is an unwritten rule that vehicles are prohibited on Tuesdays, but everyone else is allowed in. Still, the closed gate has kept me away. For one thing, every dog and walker is forced enter through a single lane that looks too narrow for Barney's comfort. And with no rangers and none of the regular activity of an open day, it has always felt too dangerous to me.

But on this day, the gates of resistance have opened. Maybe it's because I'm tired of shutting myself out. Or maybe it's because we've been walking in this park for over two years without anything terrible happening.

We skirt around the entrance median where daffodils are just beginning to bloom, and head in the direction of the gatehouse. With the road closed to traffic, the freedom to take up whatever space we want makes the park seem limitless—as if we are on the wide plains of the West. In the distance, mountains of clouds loom on the horizon.

We pass the gazebo and continue into the park. Two ospreys, the first ones I've seen all season, glide in lazy circles above us. It seems we have the whole place to ourselves for the moment, and I'm giddy with the freedom of such space. But as we approach a grassy area leading to a trail, a man and a woman with a small bulldog pop out onto the road. Immediately, I move to the opposite side to make room between us. I don't need trouble, not when we're on our own out here.

To my horror, the bulldog uses his retractable leash as a kind of land-based bungee cord, springing as far as he can across the road to muscle his way into Barney's space, which continues to shrink as I pull us farther onto the grass. The man and women with him are deep in conversation, not even watching as the little bully sputters and snorts menacingly at my dog.

I pull Barney in closer and look pointedly at the dog's owner, at the dog, then at the owner again, hoping she'll pick up on the visual clues that I need some space here. What I want to say is, *Keep your goddamn dog on your side of the road!* But because I tend to leash my voice as much as I leash my dog I don't say it. Instead, I speak to Barney, just as the obedience instructor taught me so many years ago in doggie kindergarten. *Keep the dog's attention on you. Make him look at you, not the other dog.* I pull alongside Barney, using my legs to obstruct his sight of the other dog and lean down into his face, attempting to get eye contact. Barney's eyes draw back in the direction of the dog, showing lots of white.

"Look at me, boy. C'mon, Barn. Thatta boy."

The closer I get to him, the shorter his leash gets. It makes a singing noise as it spins back into the coiling unit, whirring on the spindle until the line of cord between Barney's collar and the handle dwindles down to a few inches. I press down on the locking mechanism and my thumb stays there, skin digging into the grooved plastic. My hand grips the handle, my throat similarly rigid and tight as I lean toward Barney and attempt to speak calmly and firmly.

"Stay with me, boy. Here I am. It's okay; it's okay."

Okay, except my heart is beating a hundred miles a minute and every muscle in my body is on high alert.

I know I should relax. If Barney senses I'm scared, he will be too, but I can't help it. Panic courses through my blood. My neck tightens, my knees buckle, I continue to walk, looking exactly like a human being, but if you took a microscope to my image you would see wavy lines squiggling all around me.

We are squiggly lines. At least that's what scientists say—nothing solid, just a bunch of pulsating atoms and nucleons pulsing their way through existence, but I would bet some good money that some of us are more solid than others. Barney is all muscle and bulk, a canine Mack truck assembled from Labrador and Rottweiler parts. As for me, I suppose I'm a bird or a flower, maybe even a dandelion puff that can be blown away by a strong breeze. It doesn't take much to get my atoms shaking.

The owners of the bulldog reel him in and keep moving. The bulldog walks backward, spitting and snarling as his owners drag him past us. Barney attempts to turn his head so he can keep an eye on him, but I keep talking to him and continue walking us forward. He gives up on trying to peek around my knees and walks on, checking out what looks like a squirrel up ahead. No more pulling. No more growling. No more ruffled fur on his back. We're out of the danger zone. It's the first time Barney has ever let a potential foe get off so easily.

We continue on for a few yards before the road becomes more isolated. I turn back and head toward the entrance, feeling cautious but triumphant. For the first time, Barney has not tried to attack a dog entering his territory. And I have walked through a gate that always kept me out before.

CHAPTER 20

SPRING 2004

"DID YOU EVER TALK TO SOMEONE AFTER YOU WERE RAPED?" THE question takes me by surprise. I stare out the window of my analyst's office, a light-filled room overlooking a beautiful garden, completely unlike the room her question immediately conjures up.

"Sort of," I say. "A psychologist, I think. It didn't last long."

The rape and its aftermath is not something I often discuss in therapy, except as an aside to a question about what I was doing in my twenties or how and why I made the choices I did. In truth, the constant vigilance I maintain when walking alone and my physical reactions to certain sounds and situations is so much a part of me now that it doesn't even occur to me to discuss it. It's just who I am.

But on the drive home from the session, I start thinking about the psychologist, the "shrink" I asked my mother to send me to five months after I came home from California. She had cured my friend Susie of anorexia, and I had high hopes that she could help me. While my mother had no idea what happened in Berkeley, she knew something was wrong. I couldn't get anything together—not school, not a job, not anything except driving aimlessly

123

through the suburban streets or smoking pot in a darkened basement with my sister's dorky high school friends. So although my father's insurance money was starting to dry up, my mother agreed to pay for therapy.

The doctor's office was located in an old brick building on the university hospital campus. Though the halls were deserted, I could hear typewriters clacking from behind the row of frosted glass doors. I found the stairwell and began making my way up, feeling uneasy about being alone in the too-empty corridor. Any isolated place felt unsafe now, even a whitewashed stairwell in a medical building. Slowly, I climbed to the third floor and found the shrink's office, a small room with institution-green walls. The doctor, a thin woman who wore her hair in a tight bun, told me to take a seat and then settled in across from me with a notepad in her lap. With my back to the window, I told her how I was dragged into a garage where I flew out of my body and watched a girl who looked like me get torn to pieces from the inside out.

"How do you feel about that?" she asked.

I didn't answer. Instead, I told her how uncomfortable I felt about her staring at me and writing down notes on her yellow pad.

"I feel like you don't like me," I said.

She looked up from her pad. "Do you feel that way about everyone?"

Come to think of it, maybe I did. But that was beside the point.

She was always like this, cold and detached, examining me as if I were a bug under a microscope. I saw her one more time, maybe two before I announced that I wouldn't be back. I knew just what I needed to do to cure myself.

"And what is that exactly?" She stared at me from behind her round glasses.

"Get laid."

Nineteen and clueless, I truly believed that having sex would cure me of my problem. It was so simple a solution I was surprised she didn't suggest it. Everyone knew if you wanted to keep riding you had to get back on the horse that threw you.

About that same time, I began writing articles for a local entertainment paper. They assigned me a story on a southern rock band just starting to shake up the charts. The interview took place in a downtown hotel room with the band and a representative from their record label, an older man in polyester slacks who sat by the sliding glass doors to the balcony chain-smoking cigarettes. When the interview was over, one of the band members asked if I wanted to meet up with them backstage after the show. I shrugged and quietly said, "Sure," like it was no big deal, although I could hardly believe my good luck.

Later that night, in the big concrete room behind the auditorium at Northern Kentucky University, the lead singer presented me with a silver bracelet thrown to him by a girl in the audience. He invited me to party with the band at the Top of the Inn, the revolving lounge bar at the downtown Holiday Inn. I was thrilled to be asked.

Sitting at the bar with the band, I drank shots of bourbon chased with large swigs of Coca-Cola, and danced with the guitar player whose long blonde hair reminded me of Gregg Allman. As the night wore on, the disco lights on the dance floor began to blur, and one thing led to another. I ended up in the guitar player's hotel room taking off my top, which was actually a silky maxi-dress that I sometimes wore as a shirt. The damn thing was so long and so deeply tucked in my jeans that it kept flowing out of my pants like a magician's handkerchief. You would think I would have been more aware of the importance of what I was about to do—after all, here it was, the "cure" I'd been hoping for—but because I was drunk and stoned and glad not to be thinking too much about anything, my biggest concern was that ridiculous dress. Finally, I got it off. And then the jeans. Then I jumped into bed and cured myself of what happened in California.

Afterwards, we smoked cigarettes and talked. I loved listening to the exotic music of his southern accent. I told him I was a singer and songwriter and how tough it was to be a musician in this shitty Midwestern town. He encouraged me to keep trying. Around dawn, he walked me to my car. I asked if I could visit him on the band's farm in Florida. "You know. To jam with the band." In my mind, I wasn't a groupie, just a songwriter talking to a fellow musician. He evaded the question, asking for my phone number instead.

"Maybe I'll see you next time we come this way."

It was a direct line from one of the band's songs about picking up girls on the road. I felt stupid for all of about a minute before convincing myself this was for the best. Southern Man had served his purpose. The spell was lifted. I was cured.

Except I wasn't. Sure, I could climb into bed with men again if I were drunk or stoned enough. But it took a long time and a lot of trust before I could enjoy sex without the help of self-medication. And I still couldn't be alone outside at night or go into the woods or walk in a park unless my dog was with me. The truth was there was no alone, not for me, not anymore. My space in the world had shrunk to a very small square of safety.

In the middle of April, I wake around midnight with heaviness in my chest—emotional, fear-based heaviness—an old friend or, rather, an old enemy from long ago. I can feel anticipation gathering, the stirrings of the sleep panic returning. I lie in bed for a while, trying to breathe, to relax, wrestling with the demons gathering in the gloom above. My thoughts fly around from corner to corner, from the fear of not finishing the thesis, to being a failure as a writer, to getting old and needing Botox shots, to not having money to get Botox shots. So much to do. (*Did you remember to put the empty water bottles on the porch? Renew the library book?*) I won't be able to sleep, the old voice says, and the creeping toxicity of anxiety begins to seep through my skull when another voice says no—get up, do something different. I pull on some clothes and wander downstairs where the backyard beckons to me through the square panes of the French door.

Through the window, the lawn glows, bathed in the luminous light of a full moon and I'm pulled to it like a tide. Suddenly, Barney is beside me, probably having woken not so much to the sound of my leaving the room as the sense of my absence. We both stand before the window looking out into the night. "Want to go out?" I ask. His tail wags slowly. I open the door, and we walk out into the coolness. There's a feeling of enchantment, of things unknown, a world hidden yet plainly there.

Barney steps onto the grass, sniffing around for possums and other night creatures. But I'm held in place by the moon, transfixed by the glowing whiteness before me, the transformation of my yard from a suburban garden to a vivid, living dream. I sit on the cold, wooden boards of the deck and watch the branches of the river birch, festooned with delicate fringes of new leaves, throw dancing patterns on the grass. The stars are out, too, bright and glittering against the clear sky. Barney comes over and sits beside me, leaning his warm body against mine and I'm reminded of the line from a Joni Mitchell song—*"I am as constant as the northern star" / And I said, "Constantly in the darkness / Where's that at?*

There's something to be said for constancy. And how could Mitchell forget that light is so much brighter when it's set against a field of darkness? A few days before, I had been to a lecture by the Chinese-American author Maxine Hong Kingston where she spoke about the fire that had destroyed her home and how difficult it had been to have heart in the face of such loss. To find answers, she turned inward—meditating, being still so she could hear herself think. Finally, she understood what she had to do, what we all need to do when facing devastation. "In a time of destruction," she said, "Create something." And this, too: "Write things down, so you don't have to keep it in your body."

I wrote it down, especially what she said about Kwan Yin, the Buddhist Goddess of Compassion. Kwan Yin exists, she said, to remind us to have compassion for ourselves, for this difficult task of being human.

Recalling those words, I take in the quiet spring night and look up at the moon beaming down on me, pretending it is Kwan Yin. Closing my eyes, I let myself be filled with the light of compassion for the girl who lived in fear, the young woman who tried to forget, the woman pinned under a ceiling of panic in the middle of the night. I want to breathe in the moon, the light, the beauty of the moment.

At first, I can feel the fragile tendrils of life-affirming energy entering my body. But then something in me holds back, blocks the light as if it's fighting it. I breathe in, trying to take in the light, then attempt to breathe out whatever is reluctant to open to this luminous energy. There's a battle taking place entirely inside me as I breathe in, breathe out, entering a meditative state where I observe myself in detached fascination, as if watching from above. I relax enough to follow my breath into my body, placing consciousness in the knot of tension below my sternum. When I breathe in, there is fear. And when I breathe out, there is sadness—a very old, very resigned sadness for this inability to let go.

As I continue breathing, emotions play like musical notes in my body—the treble of struggle, the bass of sadness, the high, blistering soprano of frustration. I take in another breath, realizing that I am literally afraid to breathe.

My eyes fly open and fill with moon. I sit stunned for a long moment in the light of Kwan Yin's compassionate gaze. Finally, I'm able to acknowledge what I must have known on some level all along: I'm not just afraid of breathing.

I'm afraid of being alive.

CHAPTER 21

JUNE 2004

BY MAY, OUR WALKING SPEED HAS SETTLED BACK INTO THE RHYTHM of pre-operation days—slow but steady, no more falling, wobbly dog problems, just stopping and starting as Barney does whatever it is a dog needs to do during a fine walk on a fine day. The pace is calming, almost meditative, and when Barney stops to relieve himself on a patch of grass by the side of the road, glints of gold at the base of the sea oats catch my eye, mirrors of light reflecting the sun. Up until that moment, I hadn't realized the grasses were rooted in standing water.

I've come to realize that Barney's rest stops are becoming mine as well. While waiting for him to sniff or mark or whatever, I'm forced to stop, breathe, see and hear things that I don't notice when we're moving (even as slowly as we do on these roads). I think back to the early days of graduate school, when I used the walks as exercises to build verbal muscles of description: *sight, sound, smell, touch, taste*. Barney's longer and more frequent lingering has changed the way I move among the trees and grasses. It's an old cliché, but there is something profound about stopping to smell the roses—although with a dog beside me there's always a good chance it's not roses but something quite the opposite.

My eyes rest on a shining slick of black water pooled beneath the sea oats, and I keep them there, relaxed and softly focused. Green, reedy shoots come into view, peeking out from the base of the dried grasses. Next, I concentrate on sound and, within moments, I'm rewarded by a weighty *plunk,* the splash of a toad heard but not seen.

Barney, done with his business, moves on, sniffing the low grasses at the edge of the water as he goes. I follow his lead and take a deep breath to exercise my sense of smell. Before I know it, I'm sniffing like a dog, taking in quick, short breaths just like Barney when he's hot on the trail of a good scent. The scent I'm picking up is strong but not that good; it's a water smell, sour and slightly offensive. Stagnant? Is that a smell? I breathe in again, sniffing delicately as if inhaling the essence of a fine wine. Sulfurous—that's it—a bit like rotten eggs.

As I breathe in, the acrid, rotten-egg odor floats past my nasal passages and flips on the switch in my brain that directly connects the present with the past, taking me from a park in Annapolis to the elevated highways of Jersey City, New Jersey, where I'm driving with my father through the industrial corridor of the meadowlands outside New York City. Fire-belching smokestacks pass by at eye level as a wasteland of factories and warehouses spread out below. An awful odor fills the air, one that sticks in my throat and makes me think of bologna sandwiches that have been left in a lunchbox too long. I ask him what the bad smell is. "Sulfur dioxide," my father says. "Smells like rotten eggs, doesn't it? It's a chemical."

A child of the 1960s, I'm blissfully unaware that polluting chemicals are the reason the sunsets over the wastelands of northeast New Jersey are so spectacularly beautiful. My father challenges me to see into that sky, look at it the way a painter who works in oils does, searching out colors that keep deepening and changing—red becoming purple, then blue, then lavender, then gray. As soon as I identify one color, he asks me to look again, pushing me to see beyond the obvious, to pick out every hue, every shade possible in the palette of colors washing across the sky.

The shrieking cry of an osprey pulls me back to the park, the road, the dog in front of me. My father taught me to see the world like an artist, but somehow the artist got buried deep inside me. Now, I am pulling her back out little by little, making her see, hear, smell the world she once loved. Following Barney, I go down the list of senses again, trying to remember where I left off. *Sight, sound, smell . . . touch.* I want to touch Barney's fur, but he is too far ahead for me to reach down and pet.

A warm breeze strokes my face. The touch of a summer's day, that's what's touching me; but what am *I* touching? I become aware of my hand gripping the plastic handle of Barney's leash. It's smooth, hard, and something else . . . rounded where the handle curves in on itself. Round? Is that a touch? We walk on for a few beats and I think about it. Sure? Why not?

At the gatehouse we turn back, and the exercise begins again with the sense of smell. I'm aware of how the scent has changed on this stretch of road, from sulfurous to something sweeter, like hay or grass. When we reach the blind spot at the bend of the road, I pull Barney in, in case a car happens to come by, or worse, a person rounding the bend with a dog. This actually happened once when I was walking him with Curt, who had warned me not to walk around this blind curve. Sure enough, as we turned the bend, we came face to face with a dog and his owner. "See?" he said. "What did I tell you?"

So I am careful, keeping my eyes on every inch of the grassy strip between the road and the field next to us. We sweep around the bend in one quick movement, and at a glance I can see that it's all clear. There's nothing ahead but a tangle of raspberry canes sweeping toward the sky, but what a tangle—branches lit at such an exquisite angle by the sun that they literally glow with light. The sight stops me as abruptly as an unexpected person or dog. It's a dazzling vision—the soft, red fuzziness blanketing the canes, the fuchsia-red thorns crowned with tiny yellow flames, the flowers, white etched with pink, all so electric and alive that I hear myself say "beautiful" as the beauty enters me, becomes me, and suddenly there is no raspberry bush or me, there is only exquisite beauty. I take in a deep breath, wanting to drink it all in, when a sharp voice in my head, says *Beautiful? Why? It's just bunch of thorns.*

Suddenly, there is no sunlight, no glowing red branches, no flaming thorns, just me and my dog standing in front of an ordinary bramble bush. I'm alone and frightened. I look again, trying to re-create the vision, and I can almost see it, although I have to fight through a wall of resistance. The voice says, *There is no beauty. It's all in your mind.*

Panic sets in. I'm drowning, desperately clawing the surface of the water to come back up for air. This voice has taken me down before, stolen my joy again and again. It's that old bully, the jailer that yanks me in on a short leash when I wander too far away. But this time, instead of being reeled back I stand my ground and listen to what the voice is saying. *There is no beauty,* it whispers, *Nothing to look at, nothing that exists outside of you. No connection. Just you, alone, separate from every living thing.*

If there ever were a Devil, it would sound like this: *Don't see, don't hear, don't smell, don't touch, don't taste. Don't trust.*

Don't live.

After thirty years of listening to this bully inside my brain, I'm finally able to interpret what the voice is saying: *If you let go, if you merge with the light, the branches, the beauty, you'll disappear, end up dead like you almost did that night in Berkeley.*

It's the first time I've ever been able to listen to this message without immediately disappearing into a black hole of terror. I can almost see ether shimmering in the air, a force as astonished as I am at what has just happened.

I bring my eyes back to the raspberry canes and the field and the blue, blue sky, immersing myself in it the way I did when I was a child looking at the sunset. A feeling comes over me that eludes description, a felt sense of something I sometimes call God and at other times the Divine; the wordless, timeless, all-encompassing embrace of life itself. The panic that the voice has triggered beats against my chest and floats away. An odd silence takes over, and with it, a sense of peace. It's then I understand this argument inside me has nothing to do with beauty. It's about being safe.

As if standing outside myself, I turn and confront that shadow presence that has kept me in fear for most of my life. I hear myself say, "No. Not anymore."

Then I look at the raspberry bush. The sight of it fills me with joy. It *is* beautiful. And I am not afraid to say so.

CHAPTER 22

SUMMER 2004

I'M FUSSING WITH BARNEY'S COLLAR, TRYING TO SNAP THE PRONGS INTO THE open links to latch it closed, but the metal refuses to yield to the pressure of my fingers. My hands flutter around his neck, ever more manic in an attempt to hook up the chain while he waits patiently, smiling that *I'm going to the park* smile while I curse at the collar and order the links to *bend, goddammit,* wishing I could control this animal without resorting to choking off his very breath.

Sometimes he reminds me of a little pony, with his broad neck and tall, muscular body. He's certainly as strong as one, so strong that he has dragged me across streets while running after squirrels, slammed me into mailboxes during chipmunk hunts, and hauled me on my butt through fields for no apparent reason. The first time we ever saw Dr. Kummel, the dermatologist who initially diagnosed his chronic allergies, he pulled me down onto the floor and across a waiting room trying to get at a feisty Boston Terrier who looked at him the wrong way.

Once in the examining room, she immediately addressed Barney's behavior. "He's trying to protect you. That's what he's doing when he goes after another dog."

Whatever he was trying to do, I was beginning to sustain injuries. I admitted to her that he was just too strong for me to handle. She explained that, with a dog like Barney, the only chance I had of controlling him was to use a prong collar.

I hated the idea. "I don't want to hurt him," I said.

"Well, it's him or you."

Dr. Kummel assured me that Barney's thick neck could take whatever punishment the collar would give. "Once he learns that all he has to do to stop the pain is to stop pulling, he will."

So I gave in. I put the collar on Barney and tugged like a sailor the moment he started to run ahead of me. He yelped in pain the first few times I did it. Then, wonder of wonders, he stopped pulling.

After seven years of wearing the collar, Barney's paws dance on the wood floor in anticipation of a walk whenever he hears it jingling. He rarely pulls on our walks, and I hardly ever have to snap the leash to dig the hooks into his neck. But that doesn't mean inflicting pain to control another being is something I bear easily. Restraint by force is not what leashes were originally designed to do. The root of the word "leash" is the Latin verb *laxus*, and in ancient days referred to a rope held loosely.

But how do you do that without losing your grip?

When I was twelve, my father bought my sister and me a horse from a farmer who lived down the street. The horse's name was Danny, and he was a beauty—a palomino-colored quarter horse with a golden-red body and a blonde mane. We kept him in the farmer's barn, but the deal was that my sister and I had to groom and clean him, which, of course, I enthusiastically agreed to. Before this, I had very little experience with horses beyond movies like *National Velvet* and *My Friend Flicka*, but like most pre-teen girls, I adored them and dreamed of having one. I couldn't believe it when my father agreed to buy Danny.

He was so big that I'd have to stand on a step stool to put the heavy saddle on his back. I'd guide him to the pasture, where I'd jump up to wedge my foot into the stirrup and fling my body across his wide back, riding Western-style—directing his movements with a light, barely held bit. What I liked best was to throw down the reins, kick my heels against his rump and click my tongue, signaling him to run as fast as he could until I was no longer a girl on a horse, but a bird on a wing, soaring across the sky without caring where I was going. At one point, my parents insisted on giving me instruction in English-style riding, influenced in part by their fascination with the upper-class gentry who owned country estates in the area. I got to wear a cool National Velvet–style riding hat, but never took to the concept of holding the rein tight and bouncing up and down in opposition to a horse's natural movements. What I loved in riding a horse was the open, unbridled thrill of galloping across a field, the wild and unrestrained joy of movement.

In the barn, surrounded by the sweet smell of horse manure and straw, I'd stand on my stool and groom Danny before we went out and then wipe him down after a run, the sour fragrance of frothy, equine sweat filling my nostrils. Sometimes, I'd come in after school and just hang out in his stall, brushing out the stiff matted strands of his platinum mane until it was as straight and flowing as one of the models on a box of Clairol's Summer Blonde. I liked everything about working with a horse, except the harnessing. To get the bit in his mouth, I'd have to shove my entire hand in, forcing the steel mouthpiece between his gums until my fingers were drenched in foamy spittle and saliva. As I attached the bridle to the bit, his head would shake back and forth, the blonde mane signaling *no, no, no*—a sentiment I thoroughly agreed with.

One afternoon, I slapped a blanket on Danny, jumped on his back, and took off down the road without a harness or saddle. I don't know what I was thinking—perhaps I just wanted us both to be free. The horse ran off into an uncontrolled gallop, with me, terrified, clinging to his mane. He flew down the road, going a good mile or two before stopping at a pasture where a pretty chestnut filly grazed in the grass. Once he got to that pasture, he was unmovable. Not long after that, Danny was sold back to the farmer.

There's a delicate balance between restraint and freedom. I've covered a lot of miles in search of that middle ground.

The summer after graduating high school, my mother bought me my own car, a 1967 Ford Galaxie with bad brakes and fake leather. I used it to escape from the house, cruising down I-75 to spend time in the Clifton apartment of Steve, Bobby, Billy, and Flash, a group of guys I had met through my friend Valerie, who was already in college. I began honing the art of "hanging out" (an actual activity in those days), which mainly consisted of listening to music, smoking weed, and reading Underground comix while munching on Steve's homemade bread. Occasionally, I jammed with Flash, Bobby, and Billy, who were in a loose-knit band called the Daffadildos. Jamming was perhaps too strong a word. I strummed and sang, they grudgingly allowed me to play along. While I had a crush on Billy, nothing came of it. I was too shy to let him know.

After my first year at Ohio University, I found myself back at home for the summer. I got a job at Reflections, a rambling rock nightclub a half block from the Daffadildos's apartment, close enough that I could crash on their couch after a late night. Being a waitress allowed me to see bands like Argent and Yes for free, and though the tips weren't great, they started adding up.

One night, Valerie dropped by the club with some guys who were friends with Bobby. In between rounds of tequila sunrises and shots of vodka (which I eagerly participated in), they told me they were all leaving for San Francisco the next morning. "You ought to come," Valerie said.

I stood there with a tray of drinks in my hand, imagining what it would be like to walk the streets of Haight-Ashbury, to be right in the center of the action where the Grateful Dead played at the Fillmore and hippies danced with flowers in their hair. I had just turned nineteen. My life was mine to live. "Why not?"

The next morning, I left with just the clothes I had with me and $70 in saved-up tip money. I didn't call my mother to tell her where I was until we reached the flat plains of Kansas.

The open skies of the West made me believe in a bright and limitless future. On the western border of Kansas, the mountains rose before me like open gates, beckoning me to enter a new way of being. At a Grateful Dead concert at the University of Colorado at Boulder, crew members threw baggies of prerolled joints from the stage as everyone danced with one another. The wonders continued with each westward mile: mountains leading straight up to the clouds, redwoods towering like giants over my head. Everything was open and wide, more vivid, more beautiful, more amazing than I ever imagined a place could be.

In Utah, we stopped for the night in a deserted stretch of mountains and set our sleeping bags down on the ground. Around 2 A.M., I awakened to cold air on my face and a sky so full of stars that, for a moment, I thought I was looking out at the lights of a great city.

Once in San Francisco, Valerie and I parted ways with our companions and stayed with a blond guy she knew who was a Jesus Freak. She slept in the blond guy's bed, I slept on the couch. During the day, I took to the streets and explored the haunts of hippie legend. It had been five years since the "summer of love" and the Haight was beginning to change into something darker and dirtier. But I saw nothing of that. To me, San Francisco was the magical mystery tour come to life.

Across the street from the Jesus Freak's apartment was a coffeehouse that held an open mike session four days a week. In the evenings, I'd wander over to watch folk and blues musicians play on a small square of polished wood in front of a large window overlooking Divisadero Street. During the day, I would look into that window and see myself playing there, imagining it so vividly that for years I actually believed it was true. I could even tell you what I sang: *There is a house in New Orleans / They call the Rising Sun.*

I had found *The Rising Sun Blues* in a book of traditional folk tunes that contained a fingering chart for basic chords, which was how I taught myself to play guitar. The tune had already been made popular by Eric Burdon and the Animals, and later, Frijid Pink as *The House of the Rising Sun*, both of whom sang it from a male perspective. According to the book, though, the song was actually a woman's song, the "house" being a house of ill repute. This was my ace in the hole. I would sing the song the way it was supposed to be sung—from a woman's perspective—and gain the respect and love of an adoring public.

Only later, after I was pulled down into the currents of darkness hinted at in the lyrics, did I realize what it meant to sing about regret and loss. I continued to sing *House* but now, one line stood out for me, the warning I was too headstrong and heedless to hear: *Oh mothers, tell your daughters / Not to do what I have done . . .*

It wouldn't have mattered what my mother had told me; nothing could have stopped me then. When Valerie and I climbed into the van to head back to Ohio, I vowed I would return. And six months later, I did, galloping off like Danny in search of greener and greater pastures, not realizing I was still riding a runaway horse.

CHAPTER 23

NEXT STEPS

THE WOMAN BEHIND THE COUNTER AT THE POST OFFICE WANTS TO know if my package contains anything fragile or explosive. It's a good question. Wrapped under the cardboard and brown paper is two years of sweat and soul: all one-hundred-and-fifty pages of the thesis, the story of my band years—or, at least my attempt at telling the story. By writing about it, I've revisited years of emotional turmoil, trying to understand why I was so hell-bent on destroying myself. I'm still figuring it out. But the thesis is done. Soon it will be bound and embossed with my name on it and filed away in the university library under my name, although it is not even close to what I had hoped it would be.

"It's just the beginning," my professors say, but it also an end. In two months, I'll be walking down the aisle and out of the program. A wise friend says, "You'll find new teachers." While logically I know that's true, at this point in time the advice sounds hollow, like the "You'll find someone else" assurance given to a jilted lover.

From the post office, I drive straight to the park, leash up Barney, and head down the road. We walk and walk—past the meadow, past the playground, and around toward the meadow again. As we reach the place where the road circles back, I realize that the completion of the thesis has little to do with the loss that I feel. It's the loss of structure sending me into freefall, the sudden absence of deadlines and assignments and teachers to watch over me.

The most sobering aspect of leaving school is realizing the next steps are up to me. Before I started this journey, becoming a writer seemed like an impossible dream. and though it seems closer and even possible now, I am not sure if I'm up to the task. In my admission essay, I equated myself in my quest for an MFA to the Scarecrow in the Wizard of Oz on his—a natural thinker who needed reassurance that he had a brain. After many trying tests, the Wizard assures him that he can think as well as any of the other great minds of his time; all he lacks is a degree. A piece of paper is pulled out of a bag, the magic words are spoken, and voila, the straw man is a virtual Einstein.

When I wrote that essay I hoped to have that same storybook ending for myself. But life is not Oz. And I still have a witch or two flying over my head.

We turn to head back, and suddenly I know what I have to do. A diploma is fine, but it won't keep me going. I need to find a living embodiment of the creative spirit so I can lasso it, put my arms around it, know where to go when I'm all out of energy and faith. I need a muse. And though I have no idea what form she will take, I do know where to find her.

The park shimmers with the soft light of early summer the morning I begin the search for my muse. Barney and I take the Shark Trail up toward the swamp pond. I walk without intention, going wherever whim and dog take me. As we approach the pond, I notice a rotting tree rising out of the water, a column of pulpy wood that resembles a dripping candle more than a tree. I study the line of woodpecker holes dotting the flaky wood and the mottled shadings of color throughout. It's fascinating, but not exactly what I'm looking for.

We begin to move away from the pond when Barney pulls back, taking me closer to the water's edge. As he sniffs an overgrown thicket, I look across the road and see a scrawny but graceful willow oak bending demurely over the road.

Tall and willowy, I write later of her. Graceful in places, awkward in others. The lower branches twist and tangle with curl just like mine before I get out the hairdryer and the ridiculously large round brush to straighten out the kinks and frizz. From one angle she looks like a crone, and another, a maiden. *A wild woman,* I write, *wild and wise.* This will be my next teacher, the one to carry me to the next phase of my creative life.

Almost every day without fail, I make the pilgrimage to the Muse Tree, hoping that simply being in her presence will anoint me with inspiration. I examine her leaves, her bark, the way the wind blows her vine hair, looking for signs, messages. If for some reason our walks do not take us past the Muse, I stop and pay my respects on the way out, driving slowly, smiling and waving hello as Barney sticks his head out the window to see what the fuss is about.

On June 20th at 8:57 P.M., the longest day of the year, I clear my windowsill of its spring regalia (glass bluebird, tiny daffodil sculpture, and seed pods) and put out my summer fetishes: a painted wooden sun pin, glass dragonfly, silk butterfly, and a trio of small pink flamingos in sunglasses. I'm more than ready to walk into summer, with its long days and light clothes and late-night walks in the sweet honeysuckle air.

Barney and I head out to the park before the midday summer crowds appear. The sky is cloudless, a glorious tribute to the season on this first official day of summer. I run my fingers over one of the patches on Barney's back, trying to feel the stirrings of new fur. Just a few weeks ago, I had taken him back to Dr. Kummel to see if she could figure out why, with the Cushing's tumor removed six months ago, his hair still wasn't growing in. "Probably hormonal," she said, prescribing melatonin pills, which, combined with summer sun exposure, could possibly coax back the fur. I rub my fingers across the scratchy patch. It feels like a few new bristles have sprouted up, but I'm not sure. As we walk by the picnic area, a man sitting at a table with his wife and little girl asks me about the patches on Barney's back.

I hesitate. The long, complicated story whirls in my brain, but I can't even begin to put words to it. "Surgery," I say. He nods. I suppose it's as good an excuse as any.

141

We make our way over to the Muse Tree. Her vine-hair nods in the breeze, acknowledging my presence. I know I'm committing the sin of anthropomorphizing, making a tree into something other than a tree, but trees have been ascribed sacred powers since the days of the ancient Greeks. I recall a Zen teaching that says the way to know the true essence of a thing is to look at it without attaching any preconceived notions or labels to it.

I step back from the Muse and simply look at it, emptying my mind of "muse," "tree," anything. I notice the slim, bent frame, the brown wand of vine snaking up from the ground and wrapping around the trunk, the flowering honeysuckle threading among the branches. Higher, above the tangled mass of vine, new growth has emerged, flourishing in the sun. The leaves are more prominent, larger. It's almost as this upper half is an entirely different entity.

The older growth—the tree's past—is a complicated web of vines, leaves and branches cut off from the sun. The more recent new growth, fed by a steady diet of light, is stronger and greener than its struggling earlier self. It strikes me that it's not so different for people. We are always connected to where we have been, dragging the past behind like a trail of half-dead vines. Young branches push out of old bark, greening and growing. It is possible to make something new and beautiful and from the wrecked tangle of a life.

The first week in August I'm back on campus, this time as a graduating senior-in-residence. They assign me a room at the far end of the building that smells faintly of wood smoke and incense. It seems oddly appropriate to have been housed at the opposite end of the building from the rest of the writing program students. It's as if I'm here, but not here. After two summers of nonstop reading, learning, talking, growing, there's nothing really required of me now beyond rehearsing for the big day, hanging out at the cafeteria, and drinking wine in the evenings at informal get-togethers where an overwhelming array of bright, new students walk around with the same thrilled, scared, wide-eyed look I had when I first arrived.

With enough wine in me, I'm able to observe my professors with a more detached eye. They're no longer gods but mentors with opinions, some of which I'll take to heart, some of which I won't. It feels a lot like the growing-up process itself. I'm not yet their equal, but I no longer feel like their child, either.

On the afternoon of the graduation ceremony, I lie on the bed in the sparely furnished dorm room and become aware of a burning sensation on my neck, like a rash of some sort. But when I examine my skin under the fluorescent light of the group bathroom, it's as smooth and even as ever. It's one more strange trick my body is playing on me as I grow older: the floating dots in my vision, the lines creeping up under my eyes. I'm morphing into some other creature.

The first time it struck me that my body was not always going to be the same was when I was in my twenties. I had gotten drunk at a party and spilled flaming Sterno on my left hand. The burns were severe, but I did nothing at first besides put ice and aloe on the site, following the advice of an equally blotto medical student who offered me hits of Moroccan hash in the bathroom as I ran cold water over my hand. By the time I sought medical help, the damage had been done. My formerly perfect, smooth, postadolescence skin was marred by three raised white scars that made the back of my hand look like the surface of the moon. Over the next year, I kept looking at the hand as if it belonged to someone else. Somehow, at the age of twenty-three, I had thought I would remain the same forever. At least on a physical level.

But internally, I was all about change, swapping personas and looks like a model on a Paris runway. It took years to realize that I needed to be myself, not some idealized version of someone else. By the time I committed to the MFA program, the work was more like the job the Sterno had done—a stripping away of the layers to get to the core.

My neck is not the only thing making me itchy. It's the anticipation, the graduation ceremony rapidly approaching. I attempt to meditate, but the nervous energy is too intense, so I decide to take a walk, and head out toward one of the walking trails circling the university grounds. But at the entrance to the woods, I can't bring myself to go in without Barney. A few feet away from the walking trail is a gravel road leading to the horse stable. Since it's only a few yards away from campus, I decide to seek solace from an animal that, in my mind, is the next best thing to a dog.

The only horse in the enclosed paddock is a dark brown mare with a broad white stripe running down the center of her nose. She seems bored, lonely, swatting flies with her tail. When she sees me, she walks over to the edge of the fence, snuffling her muzzle through the wooden slats in expectation of a treat. I have nothing with me, so I pull some grass and few violets and place them in my flattened palm, welcoming the wet nuzzling of her soft mouth, the sticky goo of her spit. I could stay here forever, breathing in the perfume of manure, the smell of childhood afternoons in the pasture with Danny, but I have to go, take off my muddy shoes, and face the pomp and circumstance.

After putting on the gown and hat, I practice walking around, hoping I won't trip in my high heels over the long robe. Then I head over to the auditorium and join my class in the lobby. We all march in together, just as we've practiced, and sit in the row set aside for our program. Our commencement speaker is a famous author who also happens to be a working surgeon. He writes about the liver and the spleen and what it's like to hold a beating heart in your hand. His work informs his art, he says. His advice to us? Keep your day job (ha, ha), something none of us budding authors want to hear.

Finally, the dean calls out my name and I make it to the stage without incident, gracefully accepting my degree and walking off stage right. I return to my seat with my classmates and listen for the announcement of the winner of the Christine White award. Earlier in the year, I had submitted the essay on my father for the program's highest honor. For weeks now, I've been fantasizing about winning the award. But I have also been getting used to letting go of that hope. My essay is good, but there are stronger writers in this program. I'm not going to set myself up for disappointment.

In the darkened auditorium, the director of the MFA program introduces the award, telling the story of Christine White, a former student who met an untimely death while flying in a small plane on a tour to promote her book. I glance down the aisle at my colleagues, trying to figure out who will win the award—the girl from out west who writes about tornadoes? Or maybe the woman I've become friends with, a writer whose essays about growing up in the hills of West Virginia are infused with gorgeous lyricism. My professors huddle together in the row before me, watching with bored detachment. There are two awards given out in Christine White's honor, one for journalistic work and the other for personal essay. The director announces the winner of the journalism award first, a man who has written about hiking along the borders of the former East and West Germany. He is a great guy, and I'm happy for him.

Then it's time for the personal essay award. The winning piece, the director announces, is the story of a girl and her father. My friend leans over and whispers, "Isn't that you?" It sounds like my essay, but surely it can't be. I wrack my brain to think of another student who has written about her father. The speaker goes into more detail, mentioning New Jersey, a suicide, and other details, and slowly it dawns on me that she is indeed talking about me and my story. I can barely breathe. When my name is announced, I am stunned. The only thought in my head as I move toward the stage is—*I can't believe it.*

Afterwards, there is a reception with cheese and crackers and little tea cakes. I float up and down the lobby, feeling like a movie star as everyone congratulates me. Curt beams by my side; my teachers smile knowingly. I barely look at the sugar-dusted brownies and wedges of brie. It all seems like a fairy tale, something that happens to other people, but not me.

But it has happened to me. And it's changed everything. The last time I reached for the stars, the earth opened up and swallowed me. This time, a piece of moon was placed in my hands. My father always said the world was out to screw you, but he was wrong. Sometimes, you *can* win.

Years before, when I was still deep in recovery, I had a dream about a pair of shoes. They were gold in color but otherwise simple, business-style pumps with comfortable one-inch heels. They just stood there, lined up side by side, as if waiting for me to put them on. When I woke, the words "Step into your life," echoed in my head, as loud as if someone was in the room speaking to me. And now, I am stepping into my life, walking in the shoes that were waiting for me.

As we leave the reception, I suddenly understand what my professors were saying. This *is* only the beginning. Stepping into your life means taking responsibility for it. Now, there are no more excuses. I have to keep writing.

CHAPTER 24

FALL 2004

BARNEY LIES IN CLASSIC MOPING MODE, BODY FLAT ON THE KITCHEN floor, legs splayed out against the white tile, head immobile as his big brown eyes follow my every move: the purse hoisted over the shoulder, the drawer opening, the keys in my hand. I look over at him and shake my head.

"You can't come, B. I don't have time for a walk." He fixes his sad eyes on my face. "Okay," I say, and he immediately jumps up. "But it won't be fun. I guarantee it."

I'm going on a job interview, although my gut tells me it's a mistake. Only six weeks after graduating, Curt's company has just downsized, and I'm obsessed over not bringing in any money, even though his job is safe for now.

"Be careful," I recall a teacher warning me. "The writing time is always malleable." And it is, taking a backseat to so many distractions: laundry piled on the floor, dishes to be washed, shopping to be done, dog walks to take, weeds to be pulled, errands to run for my mother. What starts as a quick check on the Internet can pull me into the black hole of cyberspace for hours. Some days, I don't get to the writing until almost suppertime, and then it's time to cook dinner. When I don't have a good day of writing, I'm angry at myself. If I am writing, I'm frustrated at how badly everything seems to turn out.

In late September I open an e-mail newsletter and see a part-time position that looks interesting. I figure there's no harm in checking it out. I send a résumé. Within a day, I get a call and an interview date. Within the week, I put on my work clothes and have Barney wait in the car while I go in to discuss the job.

In a fluorescent-lit office, I sit across from a woman who has just been promoted to managing director of a large arts festival. She is excited but unsure of herself. It seems to me she wants someone to hold her hand, but not threaten her position.

I should know better. An insecure boss plus my background as a director of a similar event equals a potentially bad scene. But instead of me asking the questions that need to be asked, I tell her the answers I think she wants to hear. The ease at which I walk through the question-and-answer game amazes me. It's so different from the days when I was so insecure at job interviews that I could barely put together a full sentence. Maybe it's because I don't care.

We shake hands and she promises to call.

On the drive back, while Barney sleeps in the backseat, I tell myself the job is not for me, even though my past experience makes me the perfect candidate. It will take up too much time and energy. And I won't be able to attend the Key West Literary Seminar, an event I have already registered for. But when she calls me for a second interview, I say I'll be there. And when she talks salary and time requirements, I nod my head and accept. It's what I have to do. No. It's what I do. It's called sabotage. Though I no longer attend twelve step meetings, I've learned enough in those rooms to know exactly what I'm doing. *Two steps forward, one step back,* that's how change is said to happen. Well, I've just taken two steps back. Even with the affirmation of the Christine White Award, I can't let go of my belief that it's impossible for me to make a living at what I love. It's too scary to even try at this point.

After canceling my registration at the literary festival, I have troubling dreams of working in an illegal abortion clinic. I'm afraid the dream is telling me that by taking this job I am killing a part of me who is not fully born yet. In my waking hours, I push the dream to the back of my mind and proceed, telling myself it's only part-time. I just have to get more organized. Now I'm the artistic director for a large arts event *and* a writer trying to get a career started at an age when most writers already have a book or two or three under their belt. I don't have a lot of time to do what needs to be done.

The visits to the Muse become acts of desperation, frenetic attempts to convince her of the necessity and wisdom of my actions. Her answer to me is always this: *Come closer.* But that's impossible. If I do, I'll come into contact with the healthy crop of poison ivy circling the base of her trunk.

This whole park is full of *Toxicodendron radicans,* and not just the garden variety kind I remember from childhood. There are poison ivy vines, shrubs, and large-leafed and small-leafed plants. The one constant is the leaf pattern: *Leaves of three, let it be.*

The last time I encountered a patch of poison ivy I ended up with a veritable mountain range of welts all over my face, neck, and arms. I still remember what I thought was the close encounter with the weeds at grad school after my first workshop experience. So I keep a respectful distance and interpret the poison ivy as the Muse Tree's way of protecting herself, like having a fence that allows others to come only so close. Fences are a good thing; I understand the need for them, my own being rather spotty and broken in places. But at the same time, I have to wonder, what does it mean to have a Muse that keeps you at a distance?

Two weeks after accepting the job, I stand on the grassy median and admire my tree from several feet away. As I stare at the poison ivy circling her trunk, I see something that I've never noticed before: tiny thorns on the stalks of the plant. I've never known poison ivy to have thorns. Never.

On the way back to the car, we pass a park ranger fiddling with a sign. I walk over to him and stand politely behind him for a minute, watching him change the numbers on the park's closing time from 6:30 to 6:00 P.M., knowing that soon the numbers will decrease as Daylight Saving Time colludes with the waning sun to push the darkness closer and closer to 5:00 P.M.

"Excuse me," I say, talking to his back, "but is there a kind of poison ivy that has thorns?

He barely glances over at me as he answers. "Nope."

"Not even if the plant has three leaves?"

"Uh-uh. Poison ivy doesn't have thorns."

"I thought so," I mumble. He continues to fiddle with the sign, ignoring me.

"I mean, I've never seen poison ivy with thorns, but I did see a plant with three leaves that looked a lot like poison ivy except it had thorns, which I thought was really strange because poison ivy usually doesn't have thorns."

I realize I sound like a blathering idiot.

He turns around and gives Barney and me a quick once-over. "Could be a blackberry vine."

A blackberry vine. Of course.

For months, I've been wondering what it means to have a Muse that keeps me at a distance. Now I have my answer. That vine could have easily been cleared away, but instead I chose to see it as an impossible barrier. It's a classic case of approach-avoidance; the closer you come to what you want, the more you avoid it because of the fear of actually getting it. Which is probably why I took the job at the arts festival. The Muse has not been keeping me away.

I have.

At my job, I try not to care too much. I'm here for the money, to punch the time clock and save my creative energy for the writing work. But it's not in my nature to do something in a half-assed way, and in the end, both jobs suffer. Although I only work three days a week, the time I do spend working drains me so physically and emotionally that when I come home, all I want to do is eat dinner and watch back-to-back reruns of *The Love Boat*.

I'm sitting at the computer on one of my precious days off. As usual, I've waited until noon to get started. One thousand words, I tell myself. You're not getting up until that little bar in the word count section reaches four figures. But even though the word count rises, I'm not really sure that the results stack up to much of anything except sore shoulders and an aching back. Barney has been patient with me, sprawling out on the carpet behind my desk, but it's 3:30 and he's had enough. Seeing as I'm looking for a way out of my misery at the computer, I turn to Barney before the barking begins. "You win, Blubberpuss. Let's go." At the sound of "go" (the basic motivational word every companion dog knows by heart), his eyes search my face—*Did I really say what he thought I did?* When he hears the melodic ding of the computer shut-off, his ears shoot up and a big smile breaks across his face, although between changing clothes, making one more call, and getting a bottle of water, it's a good half hour before we're actually in the car and getting underway.

At the intersection of the Shark Trail and the road, Barney picks up a scent. Following the trajectory of his nose, I see something yellow and black among the leaves: a big box turtle. I've always admired the turtle's ability to retreat into protection at a moment's notice. But this guy's head is sticking out, his eyes are looking straight ahead—immobile, but defiant. I bend over to get a better look. His neck is like the skin of a rhinoceros, tough and scaly, making him look fierce for such a small animal. And he is fierce, refusing to retreat into his shell until my hands wrap around it. I pick him up, walk a few steps into the woods, and place the turtle on the leaves, turning him around to face the other direction so he won't move onto the bike path where he could get squashed or be found by children who might want to take him away from his rightful home.

It's not until I'm in the car that I realize that by moving him away from the direction of the bike trail, I set him directly on the path to the road where he could end up flattened like a turtle pancake. The thought horrifies me, but for some reason I don't turn back to find him and correct his course. I'm shell-shocked into inaction, as if some demon spirit has taped my hands to the wheel, my foot on the gas. I'm afraid that anything I do will only make things worse. It's the same way I feel about my own situation right now.

As I drive out of the park, I pray for luck and a lack of traffic so that the turtle can make it to where he needs to go. There's every possibility he'll get back on track. Or at least to the other side of the road in one piece. Sometimes, that's all you can hope for.

CHAPTER 25

SMOKE AND MIRRORS

Click, click, click. I can hear it, Barney's hip clacking bone against bone as he walks ahead of me. In the quiet of winter, the sound seems louder than it is, amplified somehow against the emptiness of the woods. Clouds thicken above, capping the sky with a nickel-gray cover, but even in this grayness, there is color: the subtle blush of rust and pink on azalea leaves, the red coat of an orange-billed cardinal, mushrooms exploding out of the ground, stark white and mustard yellow. This time of year, you appreciate the small things.

The clicking hip is a constant reminder of Barney's frailty but also of his strength; an audible sign of his persistence and will to keep going despite difficulty. The patches on his back have finally grown back, the fur thick and even, and he looks better than he has in months, despite the knocking hip bone. "As long as you can walk in this park, buddy," I whisper.

I pause, watching him totter down the road. One year ago, when he had his surgery, this is what I had prayed for. And here he is, still walking with me—my shadow, my constant friend.

When Barney was a pup, he would leap so high when he ran that he could scale three-foot fences. I called him "Joy Boy" then, because those leaps were so obviously infused with the sheer joy of being alive. But with his bad hip, there is no more leaping for Barney, except the leap he has taken to stay here and stay in the game. Suddenly, I'm filled with an overwhelming gratefulness for this moment, for every moment now that I have with him. It's easy to think that those you love will be with you forever when they're young and healthy, but the truth is, all our moments are like this, so ephemeral they can be gone in an instant.

The second week in December, we walk around the circle and duck into a small wooded trail. Since I've been working all day, we haven't been able to make it to the park until dusk, or almost dusk, and we only have ten minutes before the park will close. On our way back to the car, a flock of small birds pass silently overhead, maybe one hundred of them. It's supposed to snow tomorrow. But tonight, the sky is clear.

With twilight rapidly turning to night, I know I should get in the car and get going. But I don't. I stand there in the parking lot, lingering under a full moon hanging low over the meadow. A few yards away, a stand of saw-edged pines reach toward the sky, their ragged outlines etched in dark relief like a woodcut illustration in a children's picture book. Barney pulls his leash out and investigates the perimeter of a garbage can, but I cannot move, cannot tear my eyes away from this glorious sight until the chill air finally gets to me. I turn toward the car, then stop and look back one more time. For a dazzling instant, the moon fills my eyes like a headlamp on a dark night. Ignoring the cold stinging my cheeks, I bask in contentment, blessed with an apricot moon and a purple sky and two good legs to walk into such a sight and a faithful, four-legged companion beside me. I feel like the luckiest person alive.

But like the moon, my light wanes within a fortnight. The job is more complicated than I expected, and I'm back in one of those black moods where all I can feel is the sadness of time lost, of working with difficult people and dealing with ridiculous demands. And it's fall; the light is going, going, gone. Barney is having some tough days, too, his hip stiffening up in the cold, damp weather. There are times he is unsteady on his feet, wobbling more than walking.

Three days before the winter solstice, we begin our walk at 4:15 in the afternoon and by 4:30 the sun begins its descent. There isn't another soul out here and, with darkness about to fall, I can't help feeling creeped out. We continue walking up the road toward the Muse Tree. The fading light is infused with the soft, golden hue unique to winter afternoons. It's the first time this season I've noticed it, and it feels as if an old friend has come back after a long trip away.

I'm enjoying the light, smiling at the irony of welcoming winter, when I smell something acrid and bitter floating on the breeze. *Cigarette smoke.* I turn around to see if anyone is behind us and scan the area where the Shark Trail runs parallel to the road. Nothing.

Someone is definitely around—but where? I reel in Barney's leash, turn around, and head back to the car, forgetting all about the visit to the Muse Tree. Once we're safely in the car, I lock the doors but don't leave right away. My eyes search the woods, the gravel lot, the empty road. If I had seen the person behind the cigarette smoke, I would have been able to decide whether it was okay to stick around or not. It's the not seeing, the not knowing that makes me so uneasy.

As I look out the windshield, my eyes fall on the red blur of a cardinal sitting in a sticker bush not far from where the car is parked. I sit still and watch him. He cocks his head and looks toward the sky, listening. A few moments later, two crows land near a garbage can in the lot, just a few feet away from the smaller bird. The cardinal moves a few inches higher up the shrub. The crows scratch the ground, moving closer and closer. When they are almost in front of the sticker bush, the cardinal decides he's had enough. He flies off, leaving the troublemakers to themselves.

I have seen other birds react in the same manner as the cardinal many times in this park. When Barney and I walk by a tree or bush where birds are roosting, they simply watch us, remaining where they are for the most part, or hopping up onto the next highest branch. But when I stop and move closer—say, trying to determine whether the small bird in a tree is a chickadee or a tufted titmouse—they move away quickly, perching higher and higher until Barney and I cross a line where we become no longer objects of interest but possible predators, and they fly away.

I ponder the act of flying away, of knowing when to stay and when to leave. I had no idea how to do that when I was younger. It was like I was blind or deaf, not able to pick up on the subtle and not so subtle clues that danger might be present.

About a week before I was attacked in California, I was hitchhiking on the streets of Berkeley when two rednecks in an old Cadillac picked me up. The driver wore a ball cap over long greasy hair. The guy in the passenger seat had a long scraggly beard that reminded me of the guitar player in ZZ Top.

Before getting in, I asked them if they were headed toward campus. They said, sure, that's right where they were going. But once I got in and asked them to drop me off at University and Shattuck, they had a better idea.

"We're taking you to a party," the bearded guy said.

I explained that I couldn't go to a party. I had a job interview lined up at a poster shop. And man, did I need that job.

"Oh, you can do that later," the driver laughed.

Before I knew what was happening, we had pulled off University Avenue and onto a side street. They pulled up in front of a house and told me to wait in the car while they picked up some "stuff." The bearded man leaned back and smiled before shutting the door. "Don't go nowhere, now." I watched as they disappeared into the house.

I sat there for long minutes, actually sat in that car and did nothing. It was like I was numb or paralyzed, not even in my body. They seemed nice enough, didn't they? They said I'd like the party, right? My automatic reaction was to blankly do what I was told to do. I sat there and ignored the voice that told me to *get the hell out of there* until it practically screamed at me. Then, and only then, was I able to open the door and run away as fast as I could.

For years, I wondered why I sat there, waiting. What the hell was wrong with me? Why didn't I get out of that car as soon as the men disappeared into the house? It was only when I read about the psychology of "learned helplessness" that I began to understand.

When people are exposed repeatedly to situations that they perceive they have no control over, they begin to behave as if they are helpless even when the opportunity to avoid harmful circumstances is presented. It's like a lab rat who keeps getting shocked even when he is shown a lever that will stop it. I couldn't do anything to stop my father's violence, madness, or eventual suicide. And by the time it was all behind me, I had been so well trained that I never even thought of the options I did have to help myself: *Pull the freakin' lever. Open the damn car door. Get away from the man on the corner.*

Not surprisingly, studies have shown submissive women are more likely to be sexually assaulted than those who are not. I didn't think of myself as submissive. I thought of myself as a tough chick, a girl who could do anything and go anywhere. But underneath the ballsiness and bravado was a shell-shocked girl in a trance, a ball of fluff in a flannel shirt and ripped jeans who saw a big bad crow approach and for whatever reason—nature, nurture or just plain naiveté—didn't even think of flying away from a low-hanging branch.

Cardinals are small creatures, the males so brilliantly feathered that they can rarely hide completely. But they fly and they forage and they live their wild life among the predators that seek them out. Watching this little bird, I'm beginning to sense that staying safe does not mean shutting yourself away. There are times to sit in the sun and sing. And times when the only sane thing to do is to fly the coop altogether.

CHAPTER 26

WINTER 2005

JANUARY BRINGS A LONG STRING OF CLOUDY DAYS AS WELL AS THE surprise return of the robins who have winged their way north unusually early. I set aside a bag in the kitchen for old bread, and, when I have a good amount, I take it to the meadow near the park's visitor's center where the birds have been gathering for the past week.

I usually avoid this part of the park. The long, grassy meadow attracts a high incidence of Frisbee-tossing dog owners who can't seem to resist unleashing their dogs for a game of catch. But on this chilly, washed-out day, there's no one around but Barn and me and a couple of faded robins pecking at twigs and bare ground.

The birds scatter as we approach, settling a few yards away, resuming their hopping and pecking as I try to figure how I'm going to toss bread out of a bag and hold on to a dog leash at the same time. I hang the grocery sack on the arm holding the leash and use my free hand to toss the crumbs out. This works fine until I'm left with a large chunk of unbroken bread, which will require two hands to break into pieces.

"Hang on, Barn," I say, placing the leash unit on the ground and stepping on it to keep it in place. With both hands free, I get to work on the bread by first crunching the plastic bag between my fingers, then opening the bag and rubbing the pieces between my thumb and forefinger.

I'm so engrossed in breaking the bread into pieces that I don't see the large black dog until he's only a few feet away from us, followed by a man—apparently the dog's owner. It's obvious the animal is loose. Without thinking about it, I turn to the man, and in a loud, forceful voice say, "Get your dog. Mine isn't friendly!"

While Barney is more relaxed around leashed dogs, there's no doubt in my mind that he would still react badly if a dog entered his circle of protection. The man calls out to his companion, but the young Lab keeps coming toward us. And then something happens that I've never experienced before in this situation. Instead of the usual panic, I feel another kind of emotion—more like concerned alarm. I don't run. I don't rush to snatch the leash from the ground. I just stand there, bread bag hanging from my arm, one hand ungloved, foot standing on the leash. Barney stays where he is and looks calmly onto the scene—no fur ruffling, no low growl. He seems almost bored. I bend down and pick up Barney's leash. The dog stops midtrack and turns back to his owner.

"That's why there are leash laws," I mutter over my shoulder as I turn and walk away. Barney, who would normally be pulling in the direction of the interloper with his fur ruffled and ears set back, acts like the dog was never there.

Within minutes of the encounter, I stop wondering where the black Lab is at the moment. I don't really care. I can feel a small amount of adrenalin coursing through my body from the thighs down, but nothing like the all-encompassing heart-pounding fear an encounter like this would usually elicit. Walking on, I admire the melted-candle tree stump in the pond, the glimpses of blinding gray-white light breaking through the ceiling of clouds. I'm back to being with whatever is around me, and the ease with which it has happened surprises me.

As we continue down the road, I try to figure out what's going on. The word fearless comes to mind, not as one word, but two: *fear-less*. It's not that I'm without fear. It's just that there's less of it. The panic that usually remains in my body long after the danger has passed is weaker, holding less of a charge than it used to. And it appears the same is true for Barney. I'm not sure what has happened, but I do know this: the fear inside us is getting smaller.

Two weeks later, Barney and I sit in the fluorescent glow of the vet's examining room waiting for the doctor. I've noticed some changes in his walking, and I want to make sure he's okay. Every few minutes, Barney gets up from his flat-out sprawl position on the tile floor and walks over to the door, looking back at me in case I don't get the message.

I tell him to sit. "We're not going anywhere." Finally, the doctor bursts in through the swinging doors leading to the back rooms of the veterinary hospital. I tell him about Barney's recent bouts of unsteadiness and also that he seems to have increasing difficulty getting up from a seated position. The doctor says the cold weather might be making his arthritis worse. "Plus," he adds, "old Barney's getting up there in years." He writes a prescription for a popular brand of nonsteroidal anti-inflammation medication for canines.

That night, I start him on the drug, but I'm uneasy about it, recalling how his nose started bleeding last year right after we put him on the other brand of anti-inflammation medication. Sure enough, when I check the Internet, the research includes warnings of possible liver toxicity. Since he already has a liver condition, I call the vet and he agrees with my concerns. I'm told to bring him back for blood tests. Meanwhile, he puts him back on Prednisone, a drug that has always worked well for him but that is best used as a short-term solution.

Barney has been on and off Prednisone since he was a young pup. First he took it for the intense allergies that caused him to break out in welts on his belly. While weekly allergy shots and Benadryl helped control the worst outbreaks, he would go back on Prednisone whenever he needed additional help, usually during hay fever season. When Barney's muzzle started turning gray at five years of age, I asked Dr. Kummel if the Prednisone was responsible. "Nah," she said, "He's just one of those dogs that go prematurely gray."

It was then that I realized how much Barney and I had in common. Hay fever allergies. Going gray early. He was my dog alright.

A few days after the blood test, Barney and I are back at the vet's to discuss the results. The doctor strides in with the lab report in his folder.

"Considering his age and everything, Barney's doing great," he says. But because of the liver tumor, he decides we should stick to the Prednisone. He goes over the possible long-term effects, but I don't care. My dog will be fourteen years old in a few months. I don't even know if the phrase "long-term" even applies to him anymore. All I want is for him to be as comfortable as possible. Whatever it takes for him to walk on his own four legs.

The vet leans against the steel examining table. "You know," he says, "you're going to have to face the fact that soon Barney may need assistance getting up. He might start falling when he walks." He shows me how to place a belt or scarf under his belly to pull him up, and he tells me to make sure I carry something like this with me. "Just in case."

I watch him carefully, ask all the right questions, try the folded towel under his belly myself under the watchful eye of the vet.

"You understand he's going to eventually need your help."

"Sure," I say. "I understand." And I do. Barney is getting older and frailer. Dogs never live long enough. I know that. But I don't want to face what that means. Not yet.

When we head out to the park on a February morning, the weather is in the fifties—warmer than usual for this time of year, though rain is expected and, behind it, a cold front that will bring winter back in all its frozen fury. At the park, the robins are everywhere—massing on the field, lined up on concrete curbs, huddled together in the trees on bare branches. The scene is reminiscent of Hitchcock's *The Birds,* complete with the eerie soundtrack, except there are two distinct voices threading through the air: sweet, happy chirping and the agitated cries of alarm that occasionally sweep through the park whenever something big in the bird world is happening.

Ornithologists may have another explanation, but to me it sounds like the alarmed birds are warning the chirpers that it is too early to trust one spring-like day. A man jogs by in shorts—a happy human chirper—and I feel like admonishing him. *Silly bird.*

Amidst the din of the chatter, Barney and I enter the cut-through to the Shark Trail. As we round the bend, I see a pickup truck up ahead on the trail and some men fixing fences. Soon the clatter of hammer against steel rings through the woods in counterpoint to the cries of the birds.

Barney stops along the way and does his business, which I bag up along with a bed of clinging leaves. As we continue on, I slow down a little, and then slow down more, easing into the walking meditation I've been wanting to try out here.

I take a deep breath and a step, then another step on the exhalation, and another step on the inhale, concentrating on the entire range of motion: the backward roll of my heel, the forward motion of the ball of the foot, the slight lift of my toes, the transfer of weight onto the heel of the next foot. *Heel. Ball of foot. Toe. Heel. Ball of foot. Toe.* Moving forward, moving back.

Although Prednisone has helped Barney gain his footing again, he's quite content to move slowly, and he matches his steps to mine, checking out a bush here, a pile of twigs there, meditating the way dogs do—by completely immersing themselves in their environment. As I concentrate on the sensation in my feet, everything around me—the trees, the men working on the fence, the chattering birds—all blur into the background. I become aware that each new step, whether it's right foot to left, or left to right, begins with the motion of rolling back on my heel.

I return to the meditation, repeating the instruction *Feel the earth,* although what I feel the most is the thin layer of fuzz lining my winter boots. Somehow, this spins me into thinking about how I'm due for a new pair of boots, which leads to memories of buying these boots at a discount shoe store in Cincinnati with my mother, who bought the exact same pair, and then to wondering if she still has her boots or if she threw them out because they leak. I start fantasizing about buying a new pair when I catch my thoughts. I'm digressing again, moving not only out of my feet but out of this park, leaving the present moment to visit a Payless shoe outlet five hundred miles away. I'm struck by how similar walking meditation is to breathing meditation; whether moving or sitting, you have to keep calling yourself back. I look over at Barney, calmly absorbed in the moment, sniffing the leaves under his nose, and admire his elder dog concentration. My mind runs all over the place like a disobedient puppy.

I bring my consciousness back to the soles of my feet, except now what I feel is an annoying nub of fuzz somewhere in the vicinity of my right toe. I stop and breathe in the cool air to get centered. From out of nowhere, a firm, male voice says, "Come."

Before I can react, the sound of running steps and tinkling dog tags is at my back and a jogger whizzes just inches away, accompanied by an unleashed yellow Lab. Barney barely looks up from his investigation of a tree trunk. The man and his dog pass by and are gone. Just like that.

I'm stunned. The dog was so close that if Barney had wanted to attack all he would have had to do is lunge forward. But there was no attack. No aggressive posturing. Not even a ruffle of fur, the warning sign that signals Barney's attack mode. It's as if one of my greatest fears has just run up behind us and disappeared like a phantom.

I try to reason it out. Even with Barney's advanced age, I'm certain he still could inflict some damage on a dog if he wanted to. Or at least try. So what happened? Was he caught off guard like I was, or was my nonreaction the reason he felt comfortable enough to do nothing? I think back to Dr. Kummel's words, *He's only trying to protect you.* Maybe my fear *has* been triggering his aggression all these years.

We continue down the Shark Trail in perfect solitude. Everywhere I look, I see trees whose limbs turn and distort, kink up, twist back, dip down before growing out. Moving forward, it appears, does not always mean moving ahead. I'm aware of my feet once more, the way my body rocks back on the heel, grounding me to the earth, pulling me back and back again, always revisiting a small patch of the past before moving on to new horizons.

CHAPTER 27

MARCH MADNESS

On my day off, I sleep away so much of the morning that Barney and I don't get to the park until noon. The clouds bundle together in a snow pattern, but signs of spring are everywhere: fuzzy buds on bare branches, more and more birds in the trees. One of the most surprising discoveries I've made in four winters of walking is that budding doesn't start in the spring. The process goes on all winter long, disguised as nubby bumps on bark or dried seed pods waving in the wind. Even when it looks bleak, the cycle of growing never stops.

The tiny buds are not enough to lift my spirits. I'm still ruminating over something said during a critique at a writer's group last week, which leads me to something someone else said years ago, which leads me to feeling pissed off and frustrated all over again, mainly at myself for not saying, doing what needed to be said and done at the time. By the time I get to the park, I'm worked up inside, rehashing old e-mails and scenes, fuming internally.

I take Barney to the long end of the Shark Trail in an attempt to quiet my chattering mind. There, I turn my attention to the five senses of sight, sound, smell, touch, taste. First I notice the wide swath of dried grasses on the park side of the trail, then the magnificent old trees lining the path. A flock of Canadian geese soundlessly wing their way across the gray sky. But as we walk down the trail, my mind wanders off the path until I'm back at a restaurant picking at my quiche with the two women writers of the critique group. One of them says, "I don't think this works. It's too didactic." The other one says, "I don't get what you're trying to say. And you can't use the line "March is the cruelest month.""

"Why not?" I ask. Both of them hold their breath as if I just let go of a stinker.

"Well . . . " She pauses. "You know. T.S. Eliot? April is the cruelest month?" The woman and her friend exchange glances. As I run their comments over in my mind, I can't figure out if they are simply helpful suggestions or personal digs. The calibration of my criticism meter has only two settings: support and rejection. It's impossible for me to discern when I'm overreacting and when the perception is accurate.

I force myself to focus on the walk, on what is before me. A grotesque black growth clinging to the branch of a gnarled dogwood catches my eye. Upon investigation, I discover it's some kind of fungal formation, puffy and melted-looking like a burnt marshmallow. As we move on, a shock of white on the ground catches my eye, which, as we get closer, turns out to be mushroom-like ledges growing out of a fallen log, their ruffled edges delicately dusted with brown.

All this fungi, all this mold. Now I'm obsessed. The old biology lessons kick in, the explanation that fungus start as spores, invisible threads travel-ing on the wind, impotent and harmless until they find a weak spot like a broken root or branch where the conditions are right for colonization. Words are like those spores for me, unseen and seemingly innocuous but full of the same potential to destroy as they sail through the air and land on broken places.

As we walk I think about the phone call I got last Sunday. Curt and I were at the boatyard, scraping bottom paint off the hull of our boat, which had been hauled and put on blocks for the winter. It was cold, and I was whining about how we should have hired someone to do the work when my cell phone rang, giving me a convenient excuse to crawl out from under the boat and take a break. It was the woman who pointed out the T.S. Eliot rip-off.

"Listen," she said. "I hope you don't take this the wrong way, but Lori and I think it's best if we join another writing group. With other fiction writers."

I felt as if I'd been punched in the gut. "Okay," I said, not meaning it. I looked out over row after row of propped-up boats, their green and blue underbellies exposed in the winter sun.

"Maybe it would be good if you joined a group for nonfiction writers," she suggested.

"But you and Lori write nonfiction."

She stammered around, trying to explain how they needed to concentrate on their novels. It was bullshit and we both knew it. I wished her luck and hung up.

At our last meeting I entertained the same thought—that maybe it would be best for me to work with other nonfiction writers. But hearing her say it turned it into code for *I'm a crappy writer who isn't worth spending time on.* By the time I crawled back under the boat, scraper in hand, I was drowning in a tailspin of my own words, self-criticism aimed at the heart of my vulnerable center.

The spore has found its broken branch. Over the next few days, I feel heavy and lethargic and can't shake the feeling. I'm not depressed, I tell myself. All I have to do is to pull up my big-girl panties and move on. Instead of grieving or crying or admitting I feel like crap, I say, "Screw those two and their fiction. I don't need them."

Depression is not merely a figure of speech; it's an apt description of what it is: a sinking of spirit, a physical lowering, as if you're falling into a hole. If I was honest with myself, I would have been able to see that this state of mind actually started several weeks ago, before the constructive criticism found its way to me. Even the little things had begun to feel overwhelming: additional responsibilities at work, a simple rescheduling of a doctor's appointment, the need to schedule an oil change. Each one felt like one more straw about to break the camel's back.

And the proverbial last straw—the incident with the writers group—the floating spore landing in the center of years of self-rejection, the perfect environment for negativity to fester.

I try to get back to the work, but everything I write seems to be wrong. I write and look at what I've done and see it's not right so I go over it and then over it again before leaving it, broken and half-formed, moving on to something else that I look at later and call awful.

The material I'm working on centers around what has been a very private, almost sacred experience. In putting it to paper, I'm exposing the most vulnerable part of my life. I suppose that's why it has been so devastating to have it shot down. I stare at the words on the screen before me and wonder if I'm treading on dangerous ground here. It seems that in writing about this experience for others, I'm losing it for myself. I consider going back on the antidepressants, but it seems to me that what I'm going through is not a medical crisis but a crisis of spirit, of faith—specifically, of faith in myself.

My moody slide continues for the next two weeks. On the morning of the spring equinox, the park is covered in fog. I take Barney for a short walk and trundle back into the car. We're heading out when at the last minute I pull off into the gravel lot on the east side of the meadow. After rolling the window down for Barney, I sit there for the longest time, staring into the barren woods. The naked trees feel like old friends and I realize I'm going to miss their twisted limbs and the stillness of winter. On the back of a grocery list, I write: *The dead are good company for a heavy heart.* It shocks me to read the words, to understand, in a way I never have before, why the majority of suicides, like my father's, occur in late winter and early spring.

Just before he took his life, my father talked of other, more hopeful plans: moving closer to friends and family, reviving his old career in sales. But he couldn't do it. Now I know why. When you're in a dark place with nothing to hang on to, spring, with its promise of starting over, becomes too daunting a task to take on.

For once, I share that feeling of resignation, the dull seduction of giving in to giving up. Too weary, too empty, I don't have it in me to move on into a new season. And I don't care what T.S. Eliot or the woman from the writer's group says—here in Maryland, March *is* the cruelest month.

It's also unpredictable. If there is one thing I can cling to, it's the certainty of change. Within days, the weather turns, and it's sixty degrees and sunny. Everything looks different. The willows by the pond are suddenly chartreuse-green. Bright yellow wands of forsythia blaze around the perimeter of the parking lot. The bare twigs of tulip magnolias light up with fat buds shaped like old-fashioned Christmas bulbs. When we get out of the car, two little girls walk by dressed in pink and purple fairy princess costumes.

Everywhere I look, life is soft and pink—a sweet, airy mess of cotton candy that remains just of out of reach. It's like there's a circus in town and everyone but me has a ticket.

As Barney and I walk past the native plant meadow on the way to the Shark Trail, we pass a group of developmentally disabled young women vigorously complaining about not getting enough bathroom breaks at work. Each one is dressed in a plus-size sweatshirt of a different color—red, yellow, lavender, green. They're so engrossed in their conversation that they don't even see us. I envy their passion, their outrage, their ability to care so damn much.

Barney and I walk on, leaving their voices behind. On the trail, the hardwoods have yet to show signs of greening, although bits of color appear here and there among the groundcover. The earth has tilted, pushed into a new season. And here I am, dressed in gray and black, still struggling to move out of winter.

CHAPTER 28

SPRING 2005

ONE MONTH AFTER THE OFFICIAL EQUINOX, SPRING FINALLY ARRIVES in Maryland. It's the kind of day poets write about, when buds burst into bloom and the world seems changed on an elemental level. The sun is no longer the shy star of winter solstice; it's a glittering jewel, a bright stone swaying from a hypnotist's hand as he says, *Wake up, wake up, you are getting less sleepy.* The anchor weight of depression I've been carrying around for the last few weeks is still there, but feels lighter. Something—maybe the sun, maybe the birds (maybe the medication I started taking again)—pulls me out of my nest, lures me with sweet promises of honeysuckle and nectar. I cannot resist and, to my great relief, no longer want to. Off goes the hat. Off come the gloves. Winter memories begin to fade, and I give myself over to what is around me.

In honor of this glorious day, I bring Barney down to the paved path on the lower end of the park where the trees are all in various stages of flower. At the head of the path, I close my eyes and stand in the sun, allowing the warmth to enter me until the edges separating me from everything around me begin to fade and the hard ache I've been carrying around inside for weeks softens. When I open my eyes, they fall upon a robin hopping in the grass, her belly full, swelled with new life.

Barney looks at me, his sad, old-dog eyes saying *Can we please move on?* I look down the long ribbon of pavement toward to the spot where the trail leads to the amphitheater. Just beyond that is the dog park. I can hear the barking from here.

When we first started walking in the park, I avoided not only this trail but also the entire lower section leading to the dog park, as if it were the last ring of hell in Dante's Inferno. But now I'm thinking, why not? I look over at the large field bordering the trail and decide there's plenty of room to avoid another dog. Just down to the amphitheater, I decide. After that, we can turn around and come back.

We walk down the first part of the trail, past deep purple flower clusters of redbud trees and the milky green petals of the first dogwood blooms. At the bend, we pass two enormous shaggy-barked cedars. Barney stops to pee on the trash can under one of the trees, and I get a chance to check out the long, straight part of the trail leading toward the dog park.

To my right, the field spreads all the way to the road, providing plenty of room to spot roaming dogs and make any necessary corrections way ahead of time. On my left is a buffer of dried grass indented with several small footpaths leading to the neighborhood behind the park. I wonder if it's safe to walk past these paths, but then I see the gold trees and everything else disappears.

There are three of them—magnificent maples with yellow leaves and clusters of golden flowers glowing like the sun. As we approach, a flash of movement in one of the upper branches catches my eye. I move closer and Barney moves with me. When we're almost under the tree, we stop, both of us remaining very still. My eyes rest on where I saw the movement, focusing on golden leaves against a flawless blue sky when I detect a flash of wings. At first, it's hard to distinguish the bird from the tree. Then an outline takes shape, clearly a goldfinch—a gold bird in a gold tree and my eyes become a camera lens, seeing only the bird and the tree and the breathtaking blue of the sky. I blink and blink again, my eye a shutter holding on to the image. At first, I wish I had a camera, then realize it's not needed. This is an image to fix in the mind, a memory to keep alive.

The bird looks down at me, then looks away unconcerned, plucking at the flower cluster next to its perch. A man approaches, coming very near with a big-pawed yellow Lab puppy at the end of his leash. I move away quickly, taking Barney closer to the tree. When I look up again, the bird has gone. I can no longer find it among the gold flowers.

As we walk on, an occasional breeze ripples against my skin, gentle as puppy breath. I notice that even the trees have softened, their new growth taking on the texture and hazy look of a pastel drawing smudged in soft charcoals.

On the way out of the park, I pull the car over into a lot just before the exit, the same one I pulled into days before when I looked up at the grayness and told the sky I didn't care whether spring came or not. I take Barney out of the car and walk him over to a picnic table near his favorite spot by the woods.

Sitting on the wooden bench, I surrender to the warm sun, the soft breeze, the gentleness in the air, summoning what the Greeks call Chyros, golden moments of suspended time. I pull out my journal and pour my melted self onto the page. I write of the gold bird, the gold tree, the softness in and around me. *I have moved into spring,* I write. *You can feel God on such a day.*

Four days later, I'm back at the same picnic table. The weather has turned colder, grayer, and mistier. Like the weather, I can't seem to hold the brightness. I'm back to my moodiness and sulking, although the birds are still singing and the plants are growing, both of them happy for the rain.

That morning, before going to the park, I happened to glance at the small glass bluebird on my kitchen window ledge that my mother had given to me as a gift. "It's the bluebird of happiness," she told me before bursting into song. "Be like I, hold your head up high, Till you find a bluebird of happiness."

As I walked Barney in the rain, I thought about the bluebird of happiness and how it doesn't exist—not the bluebird, not pure happiness—except in the mind of sappy optimists like my mother. Barney, another optimist, who is still stubborn if not swift, insists that we take a proper walk, leading me onto the footpath connecting the first parking lot with the second, and then back again where we exit near the picnic table. We're standing there, catching our breath, when I look up and damn if I don't see it—an incredibly bright blue bird standing on the lower branch of a tree.

The bird is smaller than a parrot, but just as blue—the kind of bird you might see caged in a strip mall pet shop. I look again to see if it's really there or if I've just imagined it. It's there alright—the bluebird of happiness, singing just like in a corny Disney movie, sticking around long enough for me to know I'm not imagining things.

The sighting of the bird shocks me out of my ruminating gloom like cold water on a passed-out drunk. How can I deny the possibility that something greater than my own little universe of self doesn't exist when it flies into my life on the morning I have denied its existence?

I can't.

This is where the wonder kicks in, wonder at the mystery of life, at messages and signals that I believe in and don't believe in at the same time. These are the times when I know I am being pushed out into the light by some kind of divine force. It's happened before, enough that I have begun to recognize it and simply accept it. At times like this, the unbeliever in me gets pushed to the side where she sits with arms crossed over her chest, rolling her eyes as I say *I am blessed. I am grateful.* And I mean it.

A week or two later, I'm reading the morning paper, enjoying the luxury of a leisurely, ordinary day, when I am drawn to a story of an Afghani woman who found herself married to an absent husband. A young, pretty woman, she was bound in an arranged marriage to a groom who left soon after the wedding to find work in the southern part of the country. For four years, she heard nothing—no indication of his well-being, no word of his intention to return. "What am I to do?" she asked her parents. "How am I to live like this?" Eventually, she took a lover. And then one day a letter arrived saying her husband was about to come home. She ran to her beloved, spending the night with him in a dirt hut where his father discovered them. After consultation with the regional mullah, the woman was buried up to her waist in a dirt hole and stoned to death by the villagers.

Her mother said she was relieved. The girl was a criminal and dishonored her family.

As I sit at the breakfast table sipping my coffee, I am alarmed, saddened, and most of all grateful that I am not a young woman in Afghanistan. I say a silent prayer of thanks to my grandparents who brought the seed of my being to this place. At least here, I can act on the will of my heart. My fingers rest on the page. I breathe in the peace of my quiet kitchen, looking forward to a day of writing, walking, and not much else. An uneventful day. What a thing to hope for.

But the story of the young woman stays with me as I drive Barney to the park, a reminder that anything can happen at any time. A day is made of one event after another—uneven, unpredictable pearls strung on a necklace of time. Each one is different, shaped partially by action and partially by fate.

We begin our walk on the lower trail where we saw the golden maples. The leaves on the trees have turned green, but there are new sights to see: dogwoods coming into flower, bright yellow buttercups, columns of purple bugleweed rising up like miniature castle towers. Barney seems especially pleased to be back on this trail, slowly wandering back and forth, checking out a dew-covered patch of clover on the meadow before shifting over to investigate a bristly tuft of grass on the other side of the trail.

This park used to be a farm, but it's only here, where neat rows of trees line a paddock-like field, that you can see how it might have looked in the past. I decide to call this the Orchard Trail. The air is slightly nippy as we begin our walk past the trees, just cold enough to make me glad I'm still wearing a warm jacket. I'm struck by how much it feels like fall, even smells like fall. For an instant, it's as if I'm back in the autumn woods, my nostrils filled with the earthy scent of composting leaves and rotted fruit. But as I look around, the tender green of spring is everywhere, except where last year's leaves rest in winter-deep piles, ripening and releasing their perfume under the warm spring sun.

A young mother walks by, wheeling her big-eyed toddler in a blue stroller. Farther down, an elderly couple approaches, the woman leaning on a cane to walk. It's as if the seasons are walking past me in human form:

the baby in the stroller, the woman with the cane, their wobbly legs mirroring each other the same way the coming warmth of spring mirrors the waning warmth of fall. "Everything the power of the world does is done in a circle," the Oglala Sioux Medicine Man Black Elk said, "Even the seasons form a great circle in their changing and always come back again to where they were."

We walk past the redbuds and the dogwoods to the ancient cedar at the bend. Barney decides to undertake an in-depth investigation of what looks like dog urine dripping down the green metal sides of the trash can next to the tree. I stand there with him, staring up into the cedar, still contemplating the coming and going of things as my eyes rest on a pile of dead, broomstick-like branches gathered in the "Y" of the trunk. Time stretches out while Barney sniffs around the can. I continue gazing up at the tree in a pleasantly meditative stupor, not looking for or at anything.

Suddenly, the vision before me changes, shifting and reframing as if I'm looking through a kaleidoscope. The twigs become crisp and focused, taking on the form and shape of a bird's nest, the kind made of twigs and long sticks that ospreys build on the top of channel markers. It's as if a veil has been pulled off my eyes; I'm seeing something that has been there all along: not a tangle of sticks but someone's home.

As we move on down the trail, I thank Barney for his slowness, his long pauses, his moving like the old dog he is, because I never would have seen that nest if not for his pacing. Barney moves ahead carefully, almost as if stepping on needles. "Do you want to go back, Barn?" I ask. He pauses for a moment and turns to look at me, then he looks back at the trail and continues on. Slow. Cautious. But ever forward.

We're almost at the amphitheater when acoustic guitar music fills the air. It's an old bluegrass song, a tune I used to play during my college years at Ohio University when I became enamored with the music of the surrounding Appalachian countryside. We pass the band shell where an attractive silver-haired man sits on the edge of the stage, playing to the empty field. While Barney pulls his leash out and wanders off onto a patch of dried grass, I stand to the side of the trail and listen. The music is entrancing, so beautiful I can almost see little silver notes hanging in the air.

My reverie is interrupted by a loud *thwump*. When I look in the direction of the sound, Barney is flat on the ground, lying on his side in the grass like a tipped cow. I rush over to help him up, but he seems incapable of getting onto his feet. All the beauty of the past few minutes disappears and I'm as frightened as I've ever been of anything. "Please get up, Barn," I say. I put both hands around his belly and pull him onto all fours. He stands there, wobbly but erect.

I help him out of the grass to the trail. He can walk, but his left hip and leg are stiff and the movement is awkward. We move slowly. I speak to him softly, hoping my words can help, but he ignores me, acting as if this is all an embarrassing mistake he wants to forget. I head for the lawn, taking a shortcut to the car, but Barney will have none of it. He turns around and heads straight back toward the field of dried grasses, making a beeline to the same footpath he's been trying to get me to walk into the last few times we've been here.

The path is one of several similar trails leading into a scraggly patch of woods between the park and a neighboring subdivision. It looks exactly like the kind of rough, trash-strewn borderlands we used to walk, a place where the homeless might gather or a twisted predator might be hunting for women. I try and steer us back to the car, but Barney refuses.

His determination touches me, especially after the falling incident. Fourteen is a long time in dog years. Who knows how much longer he'll be able to walk? I indulge him and take a few steps into the footpath, but still within view of the park. He keeps going, and reluctantly, I follow. The grasses give way to spindly young trees and scruffy cedars before reaching a section of tall hardwoods. It's dark under those trees, and something doesn't feel right. A few yards ahead, I spot a rusted-out water heater half hidden by bramble bushes. Closer to us, about five feet away, lies an empty Corona bottle surrounded by cigarette butts. All of a sudden, I feel vulnerable and unsure of myself. What if Barney fell while we were in the woods? How would I get him back to the car? And what about me?

I think of that woman in Afghanistan again. This is America. As a woman, I can drive a car, hold a job, divorce a husband if he abandons me, and take a lover without fearing for my life. But I cannot walk into the woods or even down a city street with the same confidence as a man. In this park, I have watched young women run alone, dipping into the darkness of a trail with ease, wearing shorts and tight tank tops, the kind of clothes that are seen as grounds for rape in some countries, the clothes that some men—even in this country—consider an invitation to sex. I think of Chandra Levy, who left for a jog in Rock Creek Park near her apartment in Washington, D.C., and was found a year later as a pile of bones. And of the woman jogger in Central Park who was attacked by a pack of young men in a frenzy of "wilding." These incidents and many more like them have not stopped other women from running into the woods with their iPods and spandex shorts. When I see them disappearing into the trails, I admire their audacity, but also worry for their safety. I cannot understand how they can feel so confident running alone. Turning around, I lead a disappointed dog back to the park.

Several days later, Barney and I return to the Orchard Trail. The weather is amazing, eighty-eight degrees out, deliciously hot for May. Barney's long, pink tongue hangs out of his mouth as we round the bend by the old cedar. Just like before, he stops at the garbage can and I look up into the branches of the tree and there it is—the stick nest—cradled in the fork, exactly where it was the last time Barney brought me here. I look over at Barney. Then the tree. Then at Barney again. I can't believe it.

After our last walk around the Orchard Trail, the image of the unusual twisting branches of the stick nest had stayed with me. So I returned to the park with a camera, leaving Barney at home to rest, comfortable about walking alone on that particular section of the trail since it is fully visible from the road. I made my way down to the old cedar next to the garbage can and focused the camera on the "Y" where I saw the nest. But it wasn't there. I zoomed out, searching across the entire tree, but even under optical magnification, there was no evidence of a nest, not in any of the branches. Thinking perhaps I'd made a mistake, I walked over to the second cedar, then to the one farther down with no luck. None of the cedars had anything like the stick nest in its branches. It was as if the nest was a figment of my imagination.

But now, when I come back with Barney, the nest appears, just like that. "You're a guide dog," I tell him. And he is, a guide dog for a special kind of blind: the rushed, the impatient, the one whose vision is obscured by a head full of thoughts of things future and past.

I finger the long flowered scarf around my neck, the one I've started to take with me on our walks since Barney's fall near the amphitheater. We've increased his Prednisone dosage, and it seems to have helped, but I'm not taking any chances. Barney wanders over toward the meadow and pushes a blade of grass aside with his broad black nose. I stand there, staring, my heart so full of love for him in this moment it hurts. *Old dog,* I think as I smile at him, *Only an old dog can give you second sight.*

Barney feels my eyes on him, and he looks up, grinning from ear to ear. "You're a special guy, Mister B." He watches my face, trying to decipher what I've just said. We remain there for a long moment, me with a goofy smile on my face, he, watching, waiting, panting with that big tongue sticking out. Finally, deciding it's nothing more than that *blah-blah blather* that sometimes comes out of my mouth, he turns and ambles over to a pile of deer dung. And quicker than you'd ever imagine an old dog could be, he lowers his head and starts munching away.

CHAPTER 29

THIRD WHEEL, SIXTH SENSE

On a closed-gate Tuesday, I drive into the strip mall across the street from the park and angle into an empty space directly across from the park entrance. While I stand by the open car door fumbling with Barney's collar, a man and woman begin walking in our direction from the far end of the parking lot. There is something familiar about them in an uncomfortable way, the man holding the woman too close, the woman tense and laughing too loud. They follow us across the street and through the one open gate of the park, the smell of their cigarettes mingling with the sweet summer air.

With Barney taking his time we are slow, and it isn't long before they overtake us. Passing by, the man grins at me, reminding me of some of the men I used to know when I played in rock and roll bands—lean, careless, almost good-looking except for the cigarette-stained teeth and greasy hair. The man points at Barney as they move alongside us.

"How old's that dog? Like thirteen?"

"Fourteen," I say.

"I knew it; I knew it." He smiles at the woman. "Damn, I'm good, ain't I?"

Now they are in front of us.

The woman is less attractive close up and appears older than the man. A bedraggled redhead, her shoulder-length hair frizzes in the summer heat like a bad perm. The man stops and fingers the label sticking out of her shirt. "Here," he says as he tucks the tag inside her collar. "You look like a retard."

I can't decide what's up here, whether they are truly boyfriend and girl-friend or if the woman is a prostitute. Don't ask me why I think that. In fact, I shove that thought from my mind. *Just because she looks skanky,* I tell myself, *doesn't mean anything.* Still, the relationship is odd. She says close to nothing. He acts like a rooster with a ball cap on.

I have three choices as to where to walk when I come on Tuesdays. I can follow the road down toward the gatehouse, or veer left and take the paved path into the park, or make an immediate right into a long, wooded trail. The couple in front of us takes the wooded trail. I can tell they're not the kind of people who make regular pilgrimages to the park, but the man seems to know where he's going. And where else would you walk on such a hot day? I decide to follow them into the shade but dawdle near the entrance to the trail, walking slower on purpose so the man and woman can get ahead. We lose them and begin our walk.

The air is thick with moisture. Birds shriek high above the treetops, reminding me of the tropical rainforests in Barbados or Tobago or any of the sultry, silent places I've been where the air smells like a spice you can't identify and the threat of danger is always present. Up ahead, in a stark shaft of sunlight, the ball cap man and redheaded woman sit on a bench. We pass them by, and I nod, wondering why the heck anyone would want to sit in the sun on such a miserably hot day. *They are strange, they are strange,* I think to myself. And then think nothing of it.

Barney takes me off the trail onto a footpath fringed with poison ivy. I turn back, not only because of the ivy, but because I can see the roof of a house up ahead, which means the possibility of other dogs. It affirms my suspicion that I have to stay vigilant on this trail. It's so close to the main road that you never know what you'll find.

Barney does not want to turn around, but I direct him back toward the entrance. As we turn the bend, I see the man and woman up ahead. He is standing up and facing the bench with his shorts bunched around his knees. She is sitting on the bench, leaning in his direction, her head bobbing up and down in a staccato motion. I pull Barney back and retreat to the footpath. *Damn,* I'm thinking. *How long am I going to have to wait here?*

I suppose people have sex in the park, but in all the years I've been walking here, I've never run into it. Besides, there is something about this particular act and this particular couple that seems sordid and worse. Now I know that this was a man who went into this park with a singular intent. I could smell it on him.

From where I stand on the footpath, I can hear a bunch of kids shouting. Three boys on skateboards glide by, heading straight for the couple on the bench. They are about nine or ten years of age, wearing safety helmets and summer vacation smiles.

Under my breath, I mutter, "Look out, boys," afraid that they're about to collide with something that will change them forever. If they were girls, I might stop them, but I assume this is the kind of encounter prepubescent boys dream of having in their storied arsenal. So I let them go, glad of the racket they're making, then decide to follow. My assumption is that there is safety in numbers, even if those numbers are composed mainly of children.

The boys disappear around the bend. I wait for the ensuing mayhem, but don't hear anything out of the ordinary. Curious, I get back on the trail, where I see the man and woman up ahead in the harsh sunlight sitting demurely on the bench. The man's arm hangs around the woman as if it's Sunday in the park and how-do-you-do. I keep my eyes on the trail, wondering if they saw me seeing them.

"Sure is hot," the man says to me.

"Sure is."

Many years ago, I attended a psycho-spiritual encounter group where I was blindfolded and led into the woods by a sighted partner as part of a trust exercise. At some point, one of the other blindfolded people—a man, I could tell from his deep laughter—came up to me and began touching me in inappropriate ways, squeezing my arm, brushing my hair, not outwardly harassing, but too familiar, and strangely lighthearted in this familiarity. I didn't say anything—after all, I was supposed to trust my partner—but I kept thinking, *He's touching me the way married people touch.*

Later, when the blindfolds came off, the man found out who I was and came up to me and apologized. "I thought you were my wife."

The accuracy of my intuition made my mind spin. How did I know that this man thought I was his wife? Trust was a big issue for me. It was one of the reasons I paid $325 to undergo three days of an inspirational boot camp run by an obscure California feel-good cult. After the blindfold came off, I was as confused as ever. I still couldn't trust someone else completely—how could I? My partner in this exercise let this guy put his hands all over me. In that moment, it dawned on me that the person I needed to trust the most was myself.

Perception can be maimed as surely as an arm or leg. As a child, I was taught not see what I saw or feel what I felt. And after the attack, when I learned how dangerous it was not to be aware of my surroundings, I overcompensated, relying on fear and overvigilance. It wasn't until I was blindfolded and all I had left was that little voice that I had to listen.

He's touching you like married people do, the voice said, and when the blindfold came off, I found out that what was exactly what was happening.

I sensed there was something strange about those two back in the parking lot. If I had honored what I felt when I first laid eyes on them, I would not have followed them into the woods. I would have continued down the road, hot or not, and found another way to stay in the shade.

There is a sixth sense. It's the prick on the back of your neck when you feel like you're being watched; the sinking feeling in your belly when you know something is not quite right. It's the sense of knowing something without seeing or hearing it.

And it's about time I started using it.

CHAPTER 30

SUMMER 2005

THE LAST THING YOU WANT TO DO AFTER WALKING A DOG IN NINETY-degree weather is put him in a car that has been baking in the sun for the last half hour. So on a brutally hot afternoon, rather than park in the sun-filled gravel lot near the Orchard Trail, I pull into the one across the road where a shaded row of spaces hugs the darkest stretch of forest in the park.

As soon as I let Barney out, he reels the leash out and heads straight for a paved path leading into the woods. When I catch up with him, he's straining to get to the hollowed-out trunk of a tree. I take a few steps forward to give him plenty of snout room, peeking into the trail while he roots around. Mist-filled rays of golden light slice through the tall, green canopy and fall in diamond shapes on the paved walkway. It's breathtaking, one of the prettiest paths I've ever seen in this park. But it's narrow and twisty. I don't feel comfortable going any farther.

The next day I park in the same shady spot. Again, Barney hauls me toward the paved path and again, I follow him, this time walking in just far enough to see that the path is lined on both sides with tall, wavy trees. They are the strangest things. Magical.

Day after day, we repeat the ritual of parking in the shady lot and linger-ing at the entrance of the path leading into the forest before heading across the street to the Orchard Trail. Joggers huff by us, bike riders zoom past, couples stroll and smile as they step onto the trail. But I stay glued to our spot at the entrance, unable to join them.

Unlike the other trails we have walked in this park, this path has so many bends that it's impossible to see more than a few yards away. It's also dark and narrow. And there's something else, something hard to define. The force pulling me toward this place is powerful. I don't know whether to trust the part of me that tells me *Go ahead, walk in* or the part that says, *Stay out.*

About a week passes. The day is warm, summer-like, the air heavy with the perfume of wild roses. I stand at the entrance to the path watching the dappled sunlight dance across the forest. Birds call and chatter back and forth to one another, filling the space between the trees with an orchestra of sound. Barney pulls his leash out beyond the hollowed-out tree and wanders a few feet into the trail, looking back at me with pleading eyes.

My gaze follows the winding path, the wavy trees, the light shimmer-ing against the forest floor, and the desire to enter this path is stronger than my fear. I take a deep breath and let Barney lead me in. The twisty trees I've seen from the entrance go on forever, rising from the forest floor in undulating waves. Acres and acres of dense forest surround us on all sides. We pass groves of shining holly trees and a huge, ancient oak with knobby, amputated limbs. I have no idea where I'm going and I don't care. A bird calls out from somewhere up above. There is no answer. The quiet is so profound I can hear the trees breathe. I fill my lungs with the musky smell of forest, a memory sense from long-ago childhood. It feels like a place out of time.

Barney and I follow the dappled asphalt farther and deeper, until a patch of light appears through the trees. I assume we're approaching an open field, but as we get closer the sky widens and lightens until I can see it's not sky at all, but water, a ribbon of river sparkling in the sun. At the next bend, we take a footpath leading to a picnic spot overlooking the water. I walk up to the fence at the edge of the bluff and look out at the view. What I see is so familiar—yet so different—that it disorients me at first, spinning water and land and horizon into unorganized blocks of color and space struggling to find form. When my spatial acuity returns, I'm stunned to realize I know exactly where we are.

The river is Harness Creek. And this bluff is the sandy cliff next to the cove Curt and I have anchored out in on our boat many times over the years. While I knew this land was park property, I thought it was inaccessible, a stretch of rugged forest and wilderness so far on the edges of the property that it might as well have been the moon.

I think back to lazy summer afternoons moored here. Hours spent sitting in the sun, dipping my toes into the water as I studied the hillside, wondering how the people who occasionally appeared on top of that riverbank cliff got there. Now I know.

How strange to have traveled all this way—to the very farthest reaches of the park—only to find that it connects to the rest of my life like a missing puzzle piece.

Over the next few weeks, we keep coming back to the path I now call the Twisty Tree Trail. By now, all the landmarks are familiar to me: the entrance to the trail, the picnic pavilion at the edge of the woods, and the entrance to the other trail—the one on the other side of the pavilion. I have no idea where this other trail goes.

Curious, I find myself walking over to this trail before going down the Twisty Tree Trail, trying to determine if it's safe to walk into, but it's impossible to see very far down. Finally, temptation wins out. One morning, instead of heading back to the Twisty Tree Trail, I take Barney over to the unknown trail and walk in.

It's darker than the Twisty Tree Trail, the woods thicker, the trees taller and fuller.

We pass a stretch of deep forest on either side before coming to a place where the path dips and curves. I'm reluctant, but we press on. Patches of milky green water glint in the sun just off to our right. Through the woods, I glimpse the shallow headwaters of a creek dotted with islands of sea grass. The water is calm and still, serenity itself. Barney wants to pull off the pavement and take the footpath down to the water, but I'm not ready to leave the trail. Not until I know where it leads.

A few days later, we're back on the other path—the Twisty Tree Trail—enjoying the cool greenness of its shade. At the turnoff for the overlook, Barney angles in and beelines straight for area near the picnic table, where he promptly gets down to business. I bag up his mess, grateful that he's chosen a spot near a garbage can. When we return to the trail, rather than head back in the direction of the parking lot, I turn left and head down the part of the path we've never taken before. The move is effortless, made almost without thinking, fueled by boldness and a desire to find out where the Twisty Tree Trail leads.

The trail curves and dips sharply. It looks strangely familiar. We walk a little farther and Barney veers over to a small footpath. On my left are the same milky green waters and islands of sea grass that look like what I saw on the trail we entered from the opposite side of the parking lot. If that's so, it means the Twisty Tree Trail and the second trail on the other end of the woods are one and the same.

We keep going. Although I'm almost positive we're on the same path, everything looks different from this angle. The woods are deep and dense, but I'm not concerned. Up ahead, I see a ribbon of white that reveals itself to be a tree, then several trees: tall, elegant sycamores all in a circle, their limbs reaching out toward the sky.

I step a few inches off the trail to get closer toward the sycamores, fighting patches of bramble and wild undergrowth. Before me, the trees stretch toward the sky in towering majesty. By the time I reach the crest of the hill, I am seven years old again, walking into the woods next to our little house in the forest, where I am not a child but a princess, ruler of the magical world created in my mind.

In the distance, I see a circle of witches dancing around a fire. I study their elegant white dresses mottled with green and gray and realize that they are enchanted princesses who have been turned into witch trees. They motion for me to join them. I walk over and twine my fingers with theirs, staring up at the sky until Barney gently pulls on the leash and returns me to the woman the child has become. For a brief second, I'm disoriented as if awakened from a deep sleep.

We step back onto the paved path and continue walking until light appears at the end of the trail. Everything seems to be speaking to me now—the wind in the trees, the songbirds hidden in the lush foliage, the cry of ospreys kiting over the water nearby. I move toward the opening of light at the end of the trail. As we get closer, I see that what I suspected is correct. This *is* the other end of the Twisty Tree Trail. The two separate paths were never separate at all.

We've come full circle.

CHAPTER 31

FALL 2005

THE FIRST WEEK OF SEPTEMBER, HURRICANE KATRINA AMBLES UP the Mid-Atlantic coast, much weaker than she was in New Orleans but with enough punch to dump tropical rains and a lingering low front on the Chesapeake Bay area. Before we can even clean up the mess left behind, another hurricane glides up the Atlantic on its way to New England, bringing days and days of gray skies and sticky humidity. It's one thing after another. Just like with Barney.

First came the incident on the Orchard Trail where he tipped over on his side like a cow. Then the stumbling started, an odd mix of walking, stumbling, then walking again. Shortly after, his already unstable paw began knuckling under. And one day, not long after the knuckling, I discovered his paw bleeding—fur and skin scraped down to the tissue from constantly being dragged against the ground.

Desperate to keep him from reinjuring himself, I buy a pair of felt dog booties, hoping the fabric will provide enough protection to stop his skin from being scraped off. But the felt rips easily, with holes appearing after just a few days of walking. Then I get the idea to turn the bootie around so that the vinyl pad faces the top of his paw at the place where it knuckles under when he walks. To my relief, it works, and we're back in business.

On a mild day in late September, Barney, his bootie, and I head out for the park. During our walk, Barney's hip seems more out of whack than usual, no doubt a result of the constant dampness. I decide to take a short cut so we can pass by the Muse Tree on the way back to the car.

As we round the bend toward the pond, I scan the tree line for the graceful strands of my Muse's vine-hair, but don't see it. We get closer, almost to the pond, and there's still no Muse. I search the woods. Check my placement on the road. I look over at the pond, then across the street where the Muse should be. There's the concrete culvert and the dry stream where her roots reached deep for moisture. But no tree.

It takes a few moments before my brain registers what my eyes are seeing. There is no Muse, only a tangle of dried vines lying in the vicinity where the tree used to be. Instinctively, I move toward the vines and look for a stump, anything, one solid piece of evidence that the Muse Tree existed. Without knowing where she is, *what* she is, I'm still seeing her tall, slim trunk, the tumbling vine hair, the fragrant yellow honeysuckles studded among the branches. My brain is stuck on this image, keeps whirling around it because it has nothing else to relate to.

I push aside the pile of brush with my foot. Finally, I see a small trunk sawed level to the ground. That's it, all that's left: a raw stump, a pile of brush, a few green branches lying in the ditch.

The day I picked this tree as my muse, I was afraid of losing her. Now it's happened. The Buddha says "The teacup is already broken the moment it is made." When I first saw these words on paper, a crack opened inside me, reaching back to the day I walked out of my house and found my father lifeless in our driveway. That's what scared me when I chose this tree; it's what scares me when I love anyone, anything. Loss is the bitter twin of love, appearing in the shadow of whatever we call beloved the moment we embrace it.

My thoughts rush to Barney. I don't want to think of him as a broken teacup, but I will lose him someday, there is no denying it. I *am* losing him. I try to grasp the essence of what Buddha says about impermanence—that nothing really dies, it just changes.

Breathing in the dry, sweet smell of sawdust arising from the pile of chipped wood at my feet, it's difficult to comprehend that nothing ends, because right now, it sure feels like an end. I place Barney's leash on the ground and step on it so my hands are free. Pressing the palms of my hands together, I bow to the sawed-off trunk and the pile of vines and branches. As I stand there, I can feel the leash reeling out under my feet as Barney begins ambling toward the road. I gather some of the Muse Tree's branches and press them to my heart before leaving. When we get to the car, I'm still holding them there.

Meanwhile, the storms keep coming. I have never seen so many so close together and with so much widespread damage. Hurricane Rita races toward the Gulf Coast, threatening to flood New Orleans just as the Katrina waters have receded enough to leave the city coated in sludge. Meanwhile, in Texas a bus carrying oxygen tanks and elderly patients trying to evade Rita's wrath explodes on the highway, killing twenty-four and worsening an already horrendous mass evacuation out of the city. I believe God is spreading the pain around.

The suffering of postrecovery Katrina and the onslaught of hurricane after hurricane affects me in a visceral way. I stockpile canned goods and water like I did after 9/11 when Homeland Security suggested that everyone within a fifty-mile radius of Washington, D.C., buy duct tape and plastic sheeting to seal windows and doors in case of chemical warfare. (Although I'm not sure I would want to survive a nuclear or biological attack; dog-eat-dog is how I envision a postapocalyptic world in which man-eat-man is probably the more apt description.) Although the hurricanes are a good excuse to have canned food and bottles of water on my shelves, I suspect my obsessive shopping has less to do with Katrina and Rita than the helplessness I feel watching Barney deteriorate.

This fall, the signs that Barney is changing are too numerous to ignore: his hesitation before leaving the car, the scrambling paws on the kitchen tile when he tries to stand from a seated position, the furrowed brow as he sits at the top of the landing looking down at me, the need to cajole him into stepping onto the stairwell where I wait midway to break his fall. There is the rheumy right eye, dripping with mucus in the morning, the sagging back, the bones pushing through skin even though he eats just as much as usual. Just as I used to resist the thought of fall following summer, I want to push away the inevitability of Barney's rapid descent.

On the morning Hurricane Rita approaches the Texas coast, Barney stands at the top of the stairs pacing back and forth instead of following me downstairs as usual. Concerned, I call to him and wait to see what he will do.

Gingerly, he places one paw on the top step, then another, and then he backs off. Sensing that he is unsure, I walk back up and hold his collar as we walk together down the stairs. Two steps down, he stumbles and I have to grab him around his trunk to keep him from falling. We continue like this for the next few days, until one morning, he cannot navigate the stairs at all, and I cannot hold all of his weight, so we both slip down the last few steps and end up on our backs in the hall landing, unhurt, but just barely.

Desperate to find a more effective way to get him down the steps, I come up with a makeshift doggie elevator, a large laundry basket that can be bounced down the stairs with Barney in it. But Barney refuses to get in. Then I remember the purple and yellow doggie life jacket that we bought for him when we first got our boat. We never used it. He was just too heavy to ever get on board.

When I drape the hot, purple monstrosity over him, his body stiffens. He's not too pleased to be encased in nylon and plastic, but he allows me to fasten the clips around his belly. I grab the handle at the top of the vest and use it to hold him up as he walks down the stairs. Halfway down, his two back legs slide out under him and he slips down the stairs, taking me with him. It's a close call. I avoid a bad spill, but he's splayed on the bottom landing.

Dogs have the most wonderful way of putting the past behind them. As soon as I pick him up and take the lifejacket off, he walks stiffly to his food bowl in the kitchen as if nothing happened. When I ask if he wants to go to the park, his face breaks into a smile. So off we go. I have to help him into the car, but he's fine once we begin walking, as long as we stay on pavement where he can keep his balance.

Barney refuses to accept that he can't do all the things he used to. During the walk, he insists on going off-trail, and I have to keep pulling him back. I'd like to let him loose, just let him wander as he pleases to root through the underbrush as much as he likes. But my concern for his safety overrides my heart's desires.

At home, I head upstairs to my office to continue my writing. Barney remains at the foot of the stairs and does not bark for me to come and get him. As I work at the computer, there is an empty space at my feet, and only the *clack clack* of the keyboard instead of the soothing rhythm of dog breath.

That night, I sit at the bottom of the stairs and explain to him that he'll have to spend the night downstairs. Before retiring for the night, I give him a treat and put the doggie gate at the bottom of the steps. He gets the message, doesn't even bark in protest. As I walk up the stairs in the half-light of the hallway, the weight of his silence echoes against the walls. I feel the break—the dog downstairs, me up here—a woman without her shadow. "Goodnight, B," I say. From the darkness below, I hear Barney's tail thumping half-heartedly in response. *Goodnight.*

The morning after Barney's banishment downstairs, my husband decides to give the life jacket another try. "You give up too easily," he says. I help Barney upstairs by squatting behind him and pushing on his rear hipbones so that all he has to do is use his front paws to navigate the steps. When he reaches the top landing, on goes the purple jacket, an indignity he endures with characteristic patience. Curt grabs the handle, lifts Barney a few inches off the ground and then proceeds down the steps with his dog-shaped luggage.

As Barney's feet graze the stairs, he gets that intense look dogs get when they're swimming, when all you see are their little heads sticking out of the water as they concentrate on staying afloat. And that's exactly what he looks like: a dog swimming more than walking, his feet dog paddling half in the air, half on carpet, not stopping, intent on moving forward no matter what.

Both Curt and Barney make it unscathed to the bottom of the landing. We're overjoyed—all three of us. At bedtime, Barney goes back to sleeping in our bedroom doorway, once again the beloved black hole tripped over during midnight excursions to the bathroom. Each morning, he gets a lift downstairs with the help of a 180-pound man and a life vest that keeps its occupant floating above a sea of steps.

You can get used to anything—limping, dragging, falling, dog exiled downstairs, dog hauled down the steps in a hot purple jacket. Once the shock of change is over, the change itself becomes the norm. My husband is right—I do give up too easily. It's becoming clear that Barney is a dog with nine lives. He has his good days and bad days, and on the bad days I immediately go straight to the worst possible conclusion. This is when I have to keep reminding myself not every setback is a forever thing.

Around Halloween, I dress in orange and black and take Barney down the Twisty Tree Trail to the Harness Creek overlook. It's cool ("nippy," the cold weather lovers would say), but outside of that, an exquisite day with a shining sky washed clean of yesterday's front and brilliant sunshine slanting through the orange and reds of the trees. Fall has settled in and has made herself very comfortable, and although I have learned to appreciate the season, I'm still wary of the changes it can bring.

Since there's no one at the overlook, I unleash Barney, something I've been doing on occasion now since he's proven that he's just not as interested in (or capable of) messing with other dogs. He noses around the picnic table, then edges up to the narrow footpath following the bluff above the creek where he looks at me, looks at the path, then pointedly looks at me again. "That where you want to go?" I ask. As soon as the words leave my mouth, he turns and enters the path. I follow.

At first the trail is easily navigable, smooth and dusted with dry, sandy soil. But it isn't long before we meander into wilder territory. Tree roots push up through the soil, twigs and fallen limbs and large chunks of broken bark litter the way. The ground is uneven at best, but Barney remains remarkably steady. He takes me past a small break in the trees where the creek shimmers in the afternoon sun. This is as far as I've ever gone on this path. I hesitate here, but Barney keeps going. I watch him disappear around the bend and follow him, curiously absent of any of the fear I used to feel when starting down a new path. The trail begins to dip down, greenery and brush closing in on us. Out of nowhere, a bone-chilling screech echoes in the woods. After an initial heart-pounding episode, I realize it's just a blue heron, close by from the sound of it, but the foliage blocks any view of the sky or the bird.

Finally, we come to the end of the path, a bluff overlooking the headwaters of the creek. It's a place of such astonishing beauty it almost doesn't look real. The water is the color of Spanish olives and as still as a prayer, so calm it looks as if you could walk on it. Marsh grass with plumes of burnished steel wave in the breeze. Gold and burgundy trees shimmer in the sun on the opposite shore. Even the deadwood is beautiful, the fallen tree trunks bleached and washed bone-gray in the water, their driftwood fingers reaching out of the muck. Barney and I look out over the water, the smell of salt and swamp filling our nostrils. Suddenly, two ducks fly out from the shore below, honking and squawking as if they've had enough of the two of us.

We linger for a while, Barney sitting on the soft bed of pine needles, engaged, alert, his Labrador eyes following the ducks over the water, and me sitting next to him, stroking his fur, glad to be with him. I wish this moment could last forever, but that's impossible. We sit there, watching the water until the clouds start rolling in. I get up to leave and he follows reluctantly.

On the way back, we encounter a dead log blocking the path. Instead of going around it, Barney springs into a jump before I can stop him. I fully expect him to crash land, to have a heap of broken dog in the woods, but he executes the jump perfectly and lands on his feet. I can't believe it. I clap my hands and yell "Bravo," as he disappears down the trail. I'm elated. There's a few tricks left in the old boy yet.

The next morning, Barney sprawls across the entrance to our bedroom, oblivious to me as I step over him to get back and forth to the bathroom. "C'mon sleepy boy," I say. "Rise and shine."

He thumps his tail on the floor, a drowsy good morning greeting. Out of the corner of my eye, I see him rise and then crumple, his legs folding under him like pleated paper. Before I can reach him, he tries again, and again, then falls to the floor.

I rush over and kneel beside him. Although I'm trembling inside, I speak in a soothing voice, hoping he won't pick up on my panic. We sit on the floor for several minutes, he sphinx-like with his front legs flat on the ground, me telling him it's all okay until he stumbles on his feet again and, helped by my hands, rises up, standing. But when I release my hands from his body his feet buckle beneath him and he's once again flat on the floor.

I want to cry, but won't for Barney's sake. Curt carries him downstairs and deposits him in the den. Wrapping my softest chenille scarf around his belly, I hoist him up, just like the doctor showed me months before. With the support, he's able to walk, so I take him out back to pee, which he does without lifting his leg. Then, he just stands there, looking over his shoulder at the scarf and then at me, that old Jack Benny *puh-leese* look in his eyes.

"Alright, you win." I loosen my grip so that the scarf is around him but no longer holding him and—surprise!—he is able to stand. After a minute or two, I remove the scarf altogether and he walks toward the house, his gait stiff and awkward, but walking, thank you God, walking. My heart begins to lift a little.

In two hours we're at the vet's office. Barney appears to be almost back to normal, which means steady on his feet with that draggy back paw in tow. The doctor isn't too concerned, says he might have slept on his front leg or sprained it while leaping over the log. He takes blood to run some diagnostic tests and determine if Barney can take other drugs for pain.

Dr. Monk is Barney's doctor, but sometimes it feels like he's mine. Lately, I've become the more demanding patient—asking for reassurance, insight, something to help me navigate the dark passage of canine old age. In the sterile box of the examining room, I tell him things I might tell a therapist; about how special this dog is, how terrified I am of having to put him down, how I hope to not have to do that—and how do you know, anyway, when that time comes?

"I'm writing about him," I say, as if that explains everything.

"Well, you're not at the final chapter yet," he says, tapping the syringe filled with plum-colored blood. "At this point, I'd say keep writing." And the next day, the old Barn is back, walking on his own as if yesterday never happened.

The next week, I receive a message from the vet's office that says the results of the blood test are back. We're already at the park, so I take Barney for a short walk before phoning the vet from the car. "You've got to give this dog credit," he says, his voice upbeat. "He's a survivor."

Apparently, Barney's enzyme levels are off-the-charts high, which means the liver tumor has returned. The vet ticks off the results one by one, a series of letters and numbers that sound like a blur against the blood pounding in my ears. When he's done, I make him repeat each test, spell it out as I write down letters and numbers that I have no idea how to interpret. Finally I ask the only question that matters to me. "How long does he have?" There's a beat of silence on the other end before he answers.

"Your dog's a ticking time bomb," he says. "Every week, every month now, is a plus at this point."

I'm parked at the top of a hill near the visitor's center and can hear the doctor clearly. Usually, whenever I use the cell phone in the park it breaks up. But this time, the signal is fine; it's me that's breaking up. As I put the car in gear, the doctor's words echo in my head: "Every week, every month is a plus." It feels like he's just given Barney an "any day now" death sentence, although that's not what he said. "Weeks, months," I repeat, trying to not alarm myself any more than I have to.

As I drive out of the park I hear myself say *It seems like yesterday,* sounding like parents do on the day their kid gets on the school bus for the first time or graduates or gets married. The leaf-strewn road before me widens out into a sticky-hot parking lot in Savannah where a big, goofy puppy with a too-wide grin makes his way toward me. In some moments, there is no space between the days. You are here. And then, you are there.

Several days later, Barney and I lounge on the grass in the backyard. I breathe in. I breathe out. I try not to think of anything else but breathing in and out. It's the key instruction in meditation, which I have practiced on and off for many years and am now returning to in earnest because what I need more than anything now is the ability to stay in the moment.

Closing my eyes, I place my hand on Barney's sleeping body and change the pattern of my breath to match the rise and fall of his ribs. My entire consciousness is focused on that precious slice of air entering me, embracing it the way a dog would. I smell the sweetness of rotting fruit under the apple tree a few yards away, which takes me back to old Mrs. Ness' farm and a nine-year-old girl breathing the frothy spittle of apple mash dripping out of a cow's mouth. I can see the blond barn straw, the soft light slanting through wood rafters. Then I open my eyes and return to the moment.

Barney is still asleep, his fur glistening in the sun. When I give him a good pat, his body thumps like a ripe watermelon. Breathing in slowly, I see just how much one breath can hold: apples and cows and a watermelon dog and a mind that flits back and forth in time like bees over sweet fruit.

I am not that good at this "being present" stuff. I can only stay in the moment for a few seconds at a time. But in this moment, I am here with my dog. And for now, that's enough.

CHAPTER 32

GOING BACK

THE SKY HAS BEEN THREATENING RAIN ALL DAY WHILE I'VE BEEN driving around town taking care of one errand after another. By the time the gray clouds deepen into twilight, I'm still not done and Barney hasn't had a walk yet. "Back in a few," I tell him before dashing into the drugstore. "Then we'll take a quickie."

When I come out, the air feels wet even though it's only misting, not quite raining yet. I clip on Barney's leash and pull my hood over my head, trying to deflect whatever damage the dampness will inevitably do to my hair. Since the park is now closed, we head to the library next to the shopping center, cutting across the pine needle–covered lawn to a buffer of trees and plants dotting a small hill. Barney makes his way slowly up the hill and I follow, hoping he'll be motivated to get down to business, although this spot rarely produces a positive response from him. I've found that dogs are always interested in any kind of smell, but it takes a place where other dogs have relieved themselves to get them in the mood to deliver the real goods. I compare it to reading a newspaper while sitting on the john.

Approaching an upcoming intersection, I pull Barney back so we don't disturb the barking dog that always seems to be behind the corner fence. By now, night has fallen and the mist has thickened into full-blown fog. The sidewalks are empty. It's so like that night in Berkeley—the wet sidewalk, the close air, the fog misting under the streetlamps—that for a moment, I swear I can hear something behind us. In the brief instant that it takes for my head to swivel around, the fog closes in. I feel the noose of fear tighten around me. My head whips around. *No one else here. Just Barney and me.*

It's nothing, I tell myself. And then I say it again. *Nothing. No-thing.* A car drives by. The dull, white glow of the lights of the strip mall penetrates the darkness ahead. The fear is gone, shrugged off with a breath.

I let Barney into the car and slowly drive out of the parking lot, still absorbing the strange sense of calm in my body. The fog drifts from the road to the headlights and I drift with it, ten years and 3,000 miles away.

In April of 1994, I traveled to San Francisco for a conference. As soon as the plane touched down on the wet tarmac, I realized that it had been exactly twenty years—April, 1974—since I was attacked on the streets of Berkeley. The coincidence was eerie, seemed almost too significant to ignore. Still, I didn't plan on going back. I was here for business, nothing more. But while I took notes in hotel breakout rooms and sipped wine with other event planners, all I could think about was that place, that street, that girl I used to be. On the last day of the conference, I skipped the wrap-up sessions and rented a car.

When the concierge gave me directions he warned me to be careful. "It's not a good part of town nowadays."

"It wasn't then either," I said.

The trip across the Bay was nerve-wracking, full of narrow streets, strange highways, and uncertain exit ramps. But once in Berkeley, I felt at home. It was surprising how little things had changed in twenty years: there was the campus gate, the long main street of shops and bars, the throng of young people on the sidewalks. I flung the map from the rental car agency onto the passenger seat and drove on autopilot, following the bread crumbs of memory to this block of stores, this street corner, this stoplight, tracking location by feel more than sight. When the shops finally gave way to a residential neighborhood, I turned right off University then right again at a vaguely familiar corner. And there I was, back at the intersection of before and after.

I parked the car and walked across the street. From the corner, I retraced the steps taken on that rainy night so many years ago. It was the longest one-half block I have ever walked in my life. With each step, I felt the passage of time falling away, the strange sense of being in two places at once—here and there, now and then—until my feet led me to the exact spot where time stood still and my world disappeared into a black hole of darkness.

I remember how quiet it was that morning, cool and gray, the sky blunted with a dull ceiling of clouds. I was the only one on the street. "I'm still here, you bastard," I said. But it wasn't enough to be here. I had come to face down the past, to retrieve the part of myself that was left behind on these sidewalks. But all I found was an empty corner, a gravel driveway, and a wooden garage set back from the street. And this too: a woman who, twenty years after being dragged into that garage, still could not feel completely safe until she was back in her car with all the doors locked.

A stoplight up ahead forces me to return to the rain-slicked streets of the present. Staring at the pools of color reflected in the wet pavement, I'm suddenly aware of how steady my hands are on the steering wheel. My breath rises and falls in natural rhythm, filling my chest and abdomen with ease. The panic that usually ricochets through my body after a scare on the street is simply not there. Maybe this is what exorcism really is about: the banishment of fear from the body.

Tonight, I finally saw the ghost that has been hounding me all these years for what it is: a shadow—a reflection of darkness—not the darkness itself.

CHAPTER 33

NOVEMBER 2005

I UNHOOK BARNEY'S LEASH AND WATCH HIM SPIN OFF IN SLOW motion down the Twisty Tree Trail, sniffing a bush here, marking a tree here. There's no one around, which gives me a perfect opportunity to try a little experiment. I have no idea anymore how much walking Barney can actually tolerate. So I let him loose on the trail to see exactly how long he can walk when left to his own devices.

Barney takes his time, moving from one side of the path to the other, his bootie-clad back leg scraping the pavement. He makes his way past the Harness Creek overlook, then around the headwaters and continues to where the trail dips down and climbs back up again. He chugs on past the cut-off trail, beyond the white witch trees, and to my surprise, all the way to the end of the trail—about a quarter of a mile. When we reach the exit he keeps going, heading straight for the Holly Pavilion where he noses through the leaves by the grill, then under the tables, happily roaming until I hear the familiar crunch of leftover bones. I run over and put my hand into his mouth to pry out the bones, but he's been quick to swallow and pretty proud of himself.

"You're too freakin' much," I scold him, snapping the leash onto his collar, although secretly I'm glad to see he's still got some feistiness left in him. My hands are covered with saliva and tiny shards of bone. I wipe them on my pants, babbling on and on about what he just did, "Still munching bones, still getting into trouble, aren't you, old man?" Barney unreels the spool of leash in the direction of the parking lot, ignoring my laughter. He steps onto the grass and, before either one of us knows what's happening, boom, he's fallen on his side.

I run over and kneel down beside him. He's in obvious distress: panting in short, noisy gasps, his eyes unfocused and far away. "It's okay, it's okay, boy," I say. Two minutes, three, minutes go by. His gums are unusually pale, almost white, and my mind starts racing. He's fallen before, but this is different. I steel myself for the worst. This is it. I'm sure of it. He's really going this time, right here in the park, which, in a way, is a blessing. I stroke him and tell him how much he has meant to me, thank him for being my companion.

His panting becomes quiet and steady. I lay my hand on his ribs, expecting his breathing to stop any moment. But instead of expiring, he scrambles to his feet, shakes himself off and heads in the direction of the pavilion again, ready to check out the garbage goodies at the grill.

This is life with the ticking time bomb. Every change he exhibits—the tiredness on the trails, the paw that needs to be taped for stabilization before putting on the bootie, the little turds he occasionally leaves behind when he gets up from a sitting position in the house—I see as proof that the fuse is about to blow. And he proves me wrong again and again.

As I help him into the car, he licks my hand. I push down the knot of grief building in my chest, knowing that if I cry, I won't be able to stop. The heaviness settles inside me, making each breath feel like a chore. It's an old, familiar sensation, the way I used to feel the year leading up to my father's death.

My father told me of his plan to kill himself a year before he actually did it. He explained that he found an insurance policy that would pay on suicide, but that there was a catch. He had to wait a year before the policy would be in force.

206

Throughout that year, I tried to ignore what my father told me he planned to do, but it was impossible to forget altogether. He kept telling me details of the "plan," that the money would take care of all of us, and that we would move to Ohio to be near my aunt. It would be okay. We'd be rich, he said.

February, March and April went by. Each month, my father paid on his policy and jammed the receipts in a glass jar perched high on the top of the kitchen cabinets. When summer came, there was hope that maybe he would change his mind. But as the leaves dropped and fall approached, the insurance receipts piled higher and higher in the glass jar. My father put our house up for sale and told me I was going to have to take care of my brother and sister when he was gone. I jammed my feelings inside and pretended everything was okay. But despite my denial, a knot of dread began building in my chest, as heavy and dense as the overcast winter skies.

Once that heaviness settled in, it stayed with me. I went to school, listened to records, watched television, and went to work with my father on Saturdays. But everywhere I went that heaviness went with me. It didn't leave until he was long gone and buried. And even then, the ache would return on cloudy, hopeless days. Days like this one.

In the car, with Barney behind me, I close my eyes and breathe into the dull weight in my chest, trying not to push it away, but to accept it, something meditation practice has taught me. I focus all my attention on the feeling, imagining its shape and texture, letting go of attaching words to it, doing nothing but acknowledging what is there in a way I never could as a child. But this time, I can't seem to shake the well of sadness pooling inside me. What's happening to Barney is very different than what happened to my father, but it feels the same. Someone I love is going to die, and I can't pretend otherwise.

Barney sighs in the backseat and I open my eyes and straighten up. Looking out the windshield, I'm greeted with an astonishing sight. Across the road, lined up on a small knoll, are six red maples ablaze with every shade of red from the palest pink to orangey-red to deep burgundy. The intensity of the color is astounding. Almost all the other trees in the park are brown or faded yellow by now, but these maples have held on, waited until the last possible moment to burst into beauty.

For a moment, I forget the dull ache in my chest and lose myself in the feast of color before me, drinking in every detail, every subtle shade of color, the striking row lined up like lit candles, because I know the next time I come here the leaves could be gone. All it would take is a good storm and a gusty wind.

I glance back at Barney, at his soft gray muzzle and sweet eyes. He's a dog that has come into more color with age. When he was young, his coat was almost solid black with only tiny specks of caramel threaded through his fur. But with each year, the caramel has grown—lightening the area above his eyes, the burl on his chest, turning what was once an all-black dog into something special. He is as beautiful as a maple in its last blaze of glory.

The winds have been coming from the west all day, bringing thick clouds and the threat of rain. As we pull into the park, one, then two drops appear on the windshield. "I'm sorry, B," I say. Once again, I've spent hours writing at the computer while Barney patiently sleeps next to my chair. And once again, we don't get out of the house until it's almost too late.

It's barely drizzling, but I decide to take advantage of the shelter of trees on the Shark Trail in case the rain begins in earnest. As soon as we enter, we're enveloped by hushed silence, with just a twitter of bird call here and there. Traipsing down the path, I hear rain—or is it just the wind? Sometimes the two sound alike, the rain mimicking the wind, the wind sounding like rain on the leaves. We step out onto the road into a downpour. I pull Barney back into the woods and head back to the Shark Trail. We'll have to retrace our steps in order to stay dry.

On the way back, I see garbage on the trail that escaped me before: a green soda bottle in the leaves and a discarded price tag from a piece of woman's clothing. We leave the trail and walk onto the grass by the road where I see another piece of paper. It's a flyer with a pen and ink heron etched on the side. I pick it up and read: *Scenically located near Annapolis, Maryland, on the South River and Harness Creek, Quiet Waters Park offers natural beauty and a variety of recreational opportunities.*

A park flyer. I'd never seen one before.

I scan the list of attractions and facts about the park: *Three hundred and thirty-three acres of woodlands and open space. Over six miles of hiking/biking trails. Six picnic pavilions. Scenic South River Overlook* . . . the list goes on and on, covering all the places Barney and I have explored as adventurers making our way on our own.

On the flip side of the paper is a map of the park. *A map.* In four years of walking here, I've never held a map in my hand. This one is dirt-smudged and rain-wrinkled—the park laid out in black and white right before my eyes. I see the oval of road that Barney and I have circled over and over, the long tongue of trail leading down to the amphitheater and dog park, the rivers cradling the boundaries of this park, the entire lay of the land.

When we first began walking here, this place was as dense and frightening as a jungle. Now, I can see it all. *Paths cannot be taught,* the old Zen saying goes, *They can only be taken.* Over weeks, months, years of walking, my own map-making has been taking place: Shark Trail and Orchard Trail. Twisty Tree Trail. Harness Creek overlook. Barney and I have found our way through this park by placing one foot and one paw in front of another. These three hundred and thirty-three acres have been our wilderness, *our wildness,* as Thoreau would say, unexplored territory whose treasures could only be found by walking into the unknown. A map in the beginning would only have limited our horizons. Now it confirms them.

In the parking lot, I spy more litter—a purple and silver foil wrapper. My first reaction is scorn—*look at how people defile this place.* My second one is embarrassment. It looks just like the wrappers on the Nutri-Grain Bars I keep in my purse to stave off hunger. I bend down and unfurl the foil between my fingers. It *is* mine. It must have fallen out of the car when I opened the door. As thoughtful as I have tried to be, my presence has changed this place. How could it not? When you set out into the world, it's impossible not to leave tracks behind.

As we approach the car, I look down the road to where the Muse Tree used to be. A little farther back from where the Muse stood is a willow oak that looks like a younger, healthier version of my old muse. With the Muse Tree gone, there will be more room for this smaller tree to grow. She will have more sun. More space. New life will emerge out of the old and the face of this park will be changed once again.

A few days before Thanksgiving, I give up struggling with an essay about getting lost in the swamplands of New Jersey and ask Barney if he wants to take a walk. His face lights up at the sound of the word. As we pull into the parking lot near the picnic meadow, a disheveled man with a bottle-shaped paper bag in his hand walks across the grass. He looks like one of the homeless guys who sometimes hang out at the entrance gazebo. It's unnerving to see him here in the heart of the park.

I leash Barney up and scan the meadow, deciding to walk into the short trail leading through the woods. But as we start to move in that direction, the man turns sharply and heads for the same footpath we're heading for—the one between the first and second parking lot, the first path I ever took off the main road—the one I have always considered "safest."

I watch him disappear into the trail. There's no one else here; just me, Barney, and somewhere, very close, the homeless man. I'm not comfortable knowing this, but I'm not afraid either. The man probably wants nothing more than a hidden spot in the woods. But his presence adds an overlay of caution on my internal map of this place. The roads to this park connect to the outside world. And sometimes, that world becomes a part of this park.

My eyes fall to Barney and I see him as others must, as a very old, very frail dog. I recall one of the last photos I ever took of Sundance, how old he looked and how I didn't see it until after he was gone. This time, there's no denying: I see Barney as he is, and I also see the woman walking him.

Barney is no longer my protector. I am *his* protector. Which means I'm my protector, too. I look up at the gray sky, at the meadow and long line of road circling us and the empty, open field. It's all up to me now. I'm surprised that the realization of this change does not frighten me. Instead, I feel strangely empowered and determined to take care of both of us.

With the homeless guy in close proximity, I don't run away but I don't take us into the woods, either. We take a short walk around the meadow. The whole time we are there, I keep my eyes open for the man and listen for anything out of the ordinary. At one point, Barney squats to do his business and falls backward. I simply help him up and keep walking. I'm getting used to things like this.

We make it back to the parking lot without seeing the man again. Once in the car, I get in and get the hell out of there. I might not be as frightened as I used to be—but I'm not as naive either.

CHAPTER 34

WINTER 2006

I'M IN THE VET'S OFFICE READING A SIX-MONTH OLD COPY OF *PEOPLE* magazine (*Celebrity tattoos revealed! J. Lo's new perfume unveiled!*). Meanwhile, Barney does a little reading of his own, sniffing the air delicately until he finds the source of good news: bone-shaped vitamin tabs sitting in a bowl on the examining room counter. He can't jump up and snatch a treat like in the old days, but he makes it clear it would be nice if *someone* would. I set the magazine down and get him a treat. His teeth grind away in pure chewing satisfaction. "At least your appetite's still good," I say to him. Then he's back in the vicinity of the bowl, his eyes begging for another round.

The reason for our visit is twofold. First, there's the foot: he's been dragging it so much lately that the felt bootie protecting his paw has been wearing thin within days. Then there's the fecal incontinency, which has become an everyday, several-times-a-day occurrence. I'm at a loss as to what to do. So it's back to the vet's office, which is becoming a second home for us in Barney's old age.

The vet nods quietly as I go through my litany of woes. When I'm done and have told him everything and more, he bends to briefly checks Barney's foot and stands back up. "It's neurological," he says. "The signal from his brain isn't getting delivered all the way down to that paw." It's also the reason, he explains, why Barney is leaving behind little gifts on the carpet when he gets up from a sitting position. "It's just something that happens to some dogs as they get older."

As I listen to the vet, I'm amazed at how cheerful and matter-of-fact he sounds, so much so that the news of what seems like a serious degradation of Barney's nervous system really doesn't get delivered all the way into my brain. Is this more bad news? Should I be upset? I don't know what to make of it. So I don't say anything. I just go through the motions and nod my head. *Uh-huh.*

He suggests a splint for the leg, a plastic and Velcro orthopedic device used primarily for broken bones. I'm all for it, anything that will help Barney walk better. Then he checks Barney's heartbeat, his eyes, his ears, and announces that the old boy's doing very well. "We probably should do some retesting of his blood levels in a month or two to follow up."

I can barely speak. "A month or two? You told me this dog was a ticking time bomb."

He looks over at Barney and smiles. "Well, apparently one with a very long fuse."

Four days after the doctor's visit, the splint arrives in the mail from an online canine orthopedic company. It's a hard, black, plastic shell completely open in the front and curved on the bottom almost like the sole of a human shoe. I place Barney's foot in the splint (a little nervous that I'm not getting it right), and secure the Velcro straps across the front portion of the brace while Barney waits patiently. Then I let go. He takes a step. Pauses. Then another. The strappy tabs on the splint almost make it look like a knee-high Birkenstock sandal. He walks into the kitchen, the splint banging on the floor but holding his leg completely straight. I'm ecstatic.

Funny how this game of lowered expectations works. I'm thrilled to see him walking in a splint, something that just months ago would have plunged me into despair. I think about what the next step would be. A doggie wheelchair? One of those skateboard contraptions that ferry the entire back end? Right now, that seems like a terrible option. But in a few months, who knows?

Our inaugural walk with the splint takes place as the temperature rises to thirty-four degrees and the snow of the morning turns to sleet. Barney's foot makes a knocking sound against the ground, like a crutch, which I suppose in way it is. He seems to be taking to it just fine, even as tiny beads of ice begin to coat the path.

As we walk down the Shark Trail, the entire woods come alive with the delicate music of ice bouncing off every possible surface—the trees, the ground. At one point, it sounds like tinkling fairy bells. On the surface of it, there's not much to see—the sky is gray and colorless—but once again, the park is full of magic. We walk and I listen to the music of the sleet interspersed by the knock of Barney's splint, the two sounds interweaving in a strange, oriental symphony. I used to stay indoors during weather like this before Barney and I began our daily walks. Now, I'm out walking even when ice clatters out of the sky.

With alarming clarity I realize that I haven't just been walking with Barney all this time, I've been fighting. The park has been my battleground, the rain, the wind, the ice, my honorable foes. Not letting excuses win, not giving in to willful weakness, not heeding the voices that have said *It's too hot, too cold, you're too tired,* has built something in me I didn't know I had— determination, a strong heart. Clear intention.

I watch Barney make his way down the trail, ice falling at his feet, ignoring the knock of the splint as it bangs against the ground, not fussing, not stopping to check it out, just walking, doing the best he can with what he has. He has always soldiered on despite his difficulties, and witnessing his continued curiosity and delight in life, especially now, is a humbling experience. I'd like to think that when my time comes to confront the inevitable physical adversities of age, I'll be like him, but I doubt it. I don't know if I'm made of such strong stuff.

When we get home, I take the splint off and rub Barney dry with a big towel. I make some soup and let him lick the bowl when I'm done, noting the relish with which he goes after the last miniscule bit of food clinging to the side. He falls asleep at my feet as I work at the computer, snoring loudly in doggie contentment.

There are people I know who put their dogs down at the first sign of infirmity. Some of them say it is a kindness; a dog wouldn't want to live when he is no longer able to run or play Frisbee or chase after squirrels. I can't judge them. I can only know that Barney still seems to find enjoyment in many small things. He always wants to go for a ride, go for a walk, be in the center of the action, even if he isn't that active himself.

For me, this act of perseverance, of standing by him, is not a choice. It's a promise I made long ago when I brought home an overgrown puppy from a hot, sticky parking lot in Georgia. But there's another part of this deal that weighs on me, and that's the flip side of persistence, the grace of letting go.

Everyone says, "You'll know when it's time," meaning when it's no longer kind to persist in the face of obstacles. This weighs on the heart of every person who has ever loved a dog into old age. My prayer is that Barney will gracefully exit on his own, although I know there's every possibility he won't. *When will I know?* The question is a riddle I can't answer right now. The words of the Lord's Prayer come back to me, a prayer that I used to recite at the end of each twelve step meeting as if the words were beads on a mala strand. *Thy will be done.* That's all I can hope to know.

Sometimes winter throws you a bone, a warm day, a cloudless sky. On such a day, Barney and I head down the Twisty Tree Trail to the river overlook in fifty-two degree weather, a temperature I would consider chilly at any other time of the year, but in late January, a cause for celebration. He's having one of his good days, doing so well that I let him wander onto the footpath where he leaped over a log last Halloween. When we arrive at the river's edge, I swear I can see little gnats dancing in the air above the creek waters. The warm weather has softened the ground just enough that it gives under our feet, hinting at the moistness below. I sit and breathe in the smell of melting earth while Barney roots through a bed of pine needles. I can only imagine the smorgasbord of scents it holds for a dog—deer musk, dried dung, essence of squirrel.

I think about how impatient I used to be when we walked, telling Barney to *Hurry up, hurry up,* as he stopped for a leisurely sniff before lifting his leg higher, higher, to just the right angle before anointing the chosen area. I behaved in ways that would surely be interpreted as rude if visited on a human being—pulling him from the bushes, cutting short his explorations—the nagging equivalent of yelling *what the heck are you doing there* to someone taking their time in the bathroom. Now I know what the heck my dog has been doing there; inhaling the earth, kissing the trees, leaving his mark on the world. He has shown me how to embrace this vast and welcoming earth. It is not something that should be taken lightly.

We return to the trail from the overlook and head in the direction of the parking lot. Barney pauses as we pass the huge oak with the sawed-off lower branches that I call the Amputee. In fall, the tree is always a striking sight with its maroon leaves and a strange white fungus filling its limbless holes. Now, the holes are simply wood again. Barney turns around to sniff something on the trail, and as I pivot with him, I notice a woman several yards behind us walking a large brown dog. Upon seeing us, she immediately recoils a few steps back, her body rigid with fear as she jerks the leash tightly to rein in her dog. I recognize the stiff, shocked stance, the searching eyes, the holding back on the trail. And how could I not know that dog—the ears and tail rigid and erect, signaling the promise of aggression?

I stand there unable to move for a moment, not afraid, but not sure how to react. It's as if I am looking into a mirror, at me and Barney as we used to be. I'm uncertain how to handle this situation. What do you say to someone you know but don't know? What do you do when you see yourself in another's eyes?

I decide that the best move is to simply continue down the trail toward the exit. Glancing back, I see the woman and dog resuming their walk behind us. There is plenty of space between us, about fifty yards, more than enough to contain an aggressive dog. But then Barney pauses again, sniffing, turning ever so slightly so that he again faces the direction of the woman and dog. This is too much for her. She pulls her dog up and turns around. Just like I would have done not too very long ago.

Watching her disappear down the trail, I'm suddenly overcome with the desire to call out, "It's okay. There's plenty of room." But she's already gone. This is what she won't see: the shimmering water, the geese flying ever-higher in a perfect line, the softening clouds filled with light.

We walk around the bend, following the headwaters of the creek, where the olive-green water flashes through the trees and it all comes back to me—the sadness of those years, the recognition of all that has been lost—so much unseen, unfelt, unlived by letting fear take charge.

Barney stops and bends his head over a small sprig of a Laurel tree, green and shining in a narrow shaft of sun. I see us through the eyes of that woman on the trail: Barney slow and tottering, an easy target for a young, aggressive dog, and me, seemingly unconcerned about the bundle of trouble at the end of her leash. If only she knew the stories held inside our skin. I watch Barney lick the Laurel leaf, seeing him through the filter of my heart. So much this dog has given me, so much we have been through together. Suddenly, I'm overcome with gratitude, though I'm not sure if it's for Barney or myself or something more than the two of us—the park, the woods, or simply the soft halo of light touching an evergreen plant in winter.

After a brief warm spell, the sky cools and clouds and fills with flakes again. But the storm passes quickly, and the next day is bright and sunny. In the park, the meadows and grasses have disappeared under a fresh inch or so of snow. Everything is clean and clear and exposed against the white in such stark relief it almost hurts the eyes to look.

It's obvious how different our walks have become. My concern for Barney's comfort and safety has made me less able to focus on the natural world, although I make an effort to find it even in the briefest of moments. No matter how short the walk, I try to take away at least one thing; one smell, sight, or sound. Today it's the bright reflection of light, the gentle thud of snow falling off branches.

For Barney's sake, I stick to the cleared road, but he keeps wandering off into the median where the snow almost covers his paws. The tracks he leaves seem to be made by someone—or something else—three paw prints followed by one round depression, the dot-like mark left by the splint. Three and one: paw and not paw, dog and not dog. It's as if Barney is slowly disintegrating before my eyes. Becoming less and less the dog he used to be.

This is who he is now: one tough, persistent, guy. Also needy, cranky, obnoxious. He hates being apart from me now for any reason, and I can't really blame him. Earlier in the week, I was upstairs writing when I heard him barking for me from down below. *"Down in a minute, buddy,"* I told him, but the minutes went on and on as they often do when I get in front of the computer, the barking a staccato white noise in the background. By the time I got downstairs, Barney was on the floor in the kitchen lying in a pool of urine, unable to get up. I was flabbergasted. There had been "accidents," sure, little easy-to-clean-up messes, but never this before.

The look on his face. The worried eyes. "It's okay, I'm here," I told him, wrapping my hands around his wet, piss-covered fur, hoisting him up, then guiding him out the laundry room door to the yard to be hosed off, washed, dried, given a treat. He settled onto the carpeted safety of the hall and watched as I got down on my knees with a roll of paper towels soaking and scrubbing and drying away the problem. He seemed fine, content even. I was exhausted, drained of energy and emotion.

I'm no stranger to this. I've had other dogs that have become incontinent in their old age, but somehow I thought this would never happen with Barney—the puppy house-trained in days, the dog that could hold his bladder longer than a dog should have to. I think of how awful this must be for him. Dogs like to be clean and maintain impeccable dens. But it is what it is. Neither one of us has any control over what's happening.

I get Barney in the car, take off the splint, wipe the wetness from the road off his paws. When we leave the park I surprise myself by giving in to an idea that has been simmering for quite some time now. At the traffic light, instead of turning right to go home, I decide to continue straight down the road, take a little side trip just a wee bit out of the way. I follow the road for a mile or so, quieting the voices in my head saying *Turn around. You're looking for trouble.* At the big black dog sign, I turn into the animal shelter and creep down the long driveway. Barney sits up, curious at the animal smells in the air. I drive down to the shelter building and circle around, idling by the outdoor kennel to watch an adorable black and white pit bull puppy playing with a ball.

I'm mesmerized by this dog. He's beautiful, leaping and jumping, so full of life and puppy energy. I begin to fantasize about adopting, wondering what it would be like to bring a dog like him home, and then realize what a ridiculous thought that is. I'm in no position to take on another dog right now.

I put the car back in gear full of mixed feelings, the predominant one being guilt. "Goddammit Barney," I say, "you wouldn't let me have a backup puppy, and now look where I am."

Barney was a backup puppy once, joining my husband's dog Sasha who was the backup dog for Sundance. I've always had a dog waiting in the wings. But this time, when Barney goes, it will be different. There will be no fur-covered companion to stroke, no guardian barking at shadowy figures in the night. I'm afraid the chasm will be too deep, the house too empty, the loneliness too hard to bear. It's not that I want a replacement for Barney; I know that one animal cannot "replace" another. It's just I'm not sure who I will be without a dog.

As we leave the shelter, the car starts to fill with an awful smell and I know exactly what it is. I brake and turn around to the backseat where my suspicions are confirmed. Barney has evacuated himself in the car. He has never, ever had an accident in the car. *God*, I'm thinking, *look at what I've done. I've scared the crap out of my dog just by looking at another dog.*

I put the car into park and turn around to face Barney. "Only kidding," I say. "No one can replace you. You're my boy." Barney shifts in his seat, trying to avoid the mess, but only makes it worse. His fur is matted with squashed shit.

Desperate, I search the car for a doggie bag, but there's not a single one, not even in the trunk. The smell is overwhelming now. There's nothing to do but lower the windows and hope for green lights all the way home. As the cold air snaps at my skin, I spend the two-mile drive jabbering to Barney and myself, laughing, then crying, then simply shaking my head at the absurdity of it.

"Well boy," I say. "You're still the little shit I've always loved." And he is.

CHAPTER 35

FEBRUARY 2006

I'M LOST IN A LONG LINE OF WORDS WHEN A SOFT NOSE NUDGES MY thigh. Looking down, Barney's almond-colored eyes stare up at me, pleading under a furrowed brow. "Soon," I say, resting my palm on the broad, flat space between Barney's ears. He pushes his head into my hand, talking back without saying a word.

Touch is our primary form of communication. If I ignore Barney for too long, he'll wiggle his head under my unoccupied hand, flipping the palm up and down in a kind of "auto-pet" motion. If the hand is busy, he'll back up into me, offering a wiggling rear-end. Sometimes he will simply come over and lean against me. Not that he has to work that hard to get my attention. I'm always reaching out to him.

Between humans, touch is loaded with emotional baggage: sexual implications, boundaries crossed, signals misinterpreted. It's rare to be able to touch another being in a purely tactile way without any response needed or expectations conveyed, especially if you're a women. Maybe this is why pets are so important in so many women's lives.

The benefits of canine-human interaction have been acknowledged by science: simply put, petting a dog lowers heart rate and raises parasympathetic neural activity. And even more telling, studies have shown that the stronger the bond between human and animal, the greater the health benefits. This is no surprise to any of us who have loved an animal companion. We touch them and we know we are not alone.

Now his head is in my lap, a gentle but insistent reminder that I need to pay attention. I'd like to finish this essay, get it ready to send out to a journal or magazine, but the little clock in the corner of my computer screen reads 4:12 P.M. The dog is absolutely right. If we don't leave now we'll miss our chance to walk in the park on this absurdly warm winter day. I close the computer, grateful Barney is still around to push me out the door.

In the park, people are everywhere—skateboarding in shorts, playing Frisbee with their dogs, jogging—all drawn by the sixty-degree temperatures and the novelty of a coatless day in early February. Wary of winter, I'm still wearing my coat. And hat. But the weather is fine enough out to roll the windows all the way down and let the sweet, fresh air wash over us.

As I pull into the gravel lot near the Orchard Trail, my eyes are drawn to a stand of tulip poplars on the hill bathed in the soft afternoon light of late winter. The glow emanating from the bark is mesmerizing and I can't stop looking, even after turning the car engine off. The light appears as if it's not merely falling on the trees but being received by them and returned outward—an osmotic communion of sorts. For a moment, I feel peace and strength filling me almost as if I am one of those trees.

Barney shifts his weight against the dog-blanketed backseat, waiting patiently. Reluctantly, I tear myself away from the tulip trees and collect the things we need for our walk: the plastic bag, the keys, the felt bootie and black plastic splint. I snap on the prong collar (although he no longer needs such a thing) before placing Barney's paw in the splint. He's impatient, but accommodating as I wrangle with the straps, wriggling his body as if to say *Hurry up, let's get going.* The park will close in less than half an hour. There's a lot to do and not a whole lot of time to do it.

We walk through a field still green from a mild winter and make our way toward the trail where dogwoods and cedars huddle in gossipy groups.

It feels like a spring day, the ground damp and soft, the air cooling as the afternoon light falls, and the dog I'm with perky as a pup—at least as perky as a fourteen-year-old Labweiler with a bum leg and bad hip can be. Barney noses through the stiff grass in pursuit of a good smell and stops abruptly, gulping a crunchy morsel of some other dog's droppings before I can get at him. He seems to have resurrected his feces-eating habit late in life and I don't have the heart to fight it.

I tug the leash just hard enough to pull him from his find and guide us toward the trail. Up ahead, the late afternoon sun spills liquid gold over the uppermost branches of the poplars, their tapered cones rising toward the sky like spires on a cathedral. As Barney busies himself with the scents of the softening ground, the fattening buds of a dogwood tree stops me in my tracks. My eyes move upward, delighting in the stark contrast of branches and buds against a cloudless sky. "Beautiful," I say out loud.

A man walking from the opposite direction approaches us. He is older, maybe in his early sixties, with a ball cap and work boots and close-cropped hair, looking nothing like the typical recreational walker of park trails. I am surprised at how calm I am as he comes closer, how natural it is becoming for me to trust my own instincts and wait to react until I get the information needed to decide what my next move will be. As the man comes into view, his features soften and his demeanor is friendly. My radar blips back to normal, and I smile back when he grins at Barney and me.

"Something on your foot, huh, boy?" He slows down as he passes us and looks carefully at the splint. "I bet that's not fun."

I glance down at Barney, bravely hobbling along. "Oh, it's not too bad. Keeps him walking."

"Well, just as long as it's temporary." He winks at us and heads up the hill.

His words fall on me like night. It's not temporary. This is as good as it's going to get. We walk back through the field toward the car. I take off the leash, the prong collar, and the splint, and I let Barney loose in the field. He wanders lamely in a circle, no doubt looking for turds again. He is stubborn, my old dog—always wants to keep going, no matter how difficult it is for him.

Watching him root among the grasses, I'm suddenly overcome with a flood of emotion. It doesn't take much to make me feel this way lately. I'm so aware of the fragility of his life, of the limited time we have together. But along with the sadness, there is something else; I can sense it, a softening both painful and beautiful. Wave after wave of sensation washes over me: the candy-apple sweetness of fermenting leaves on the ground, the sudden coolness in the air, the glow of sunset on the field, the dog inhaling the earth, the sharp calls of the crows settling in for the night. I'm almost dizzy with it all, and I realize that for the last few months, as hard as it's been, I've never felt so alive. Walking with Barney on this last leg of his path has brought a gift beyond all gifts—a heightened appreciation for life and a deepening ability to experience it.

"As long as it's temporary," the man said. And actually, he's right. It *is* temporary. That's what makes every little thing so special to me now, from stroking Barney's velvety ears to the golden light on the trees. In some ways, it's as if I'm the one who has been told I have only so long to live instead of my dog. Each moment is felt more fully in his presence because it may be the last. This makes our time together bittersweet: precious and sad, but also filled with a grace that so easily eludes me in the more ordinary moments of my life.

I gaze up at the tulip poplars on the hill. By now, their golden halo has become paler, laced with a touch of rose-pink. The sun has moved across the road and into the woods, where a red glow burns on the horizon behind a darkened fringe of trees. Walking over to Barney, I put my hand on his collar and step forward but he refuses to budge. The fragrance of soft earth and scented grass surrounds us. It's so like a spring day that my mind reels forward, wondering if he'll be with me when the fields green again for real.

"Just a few minutes more," I say, releasing him. The sun is fast disappearing in the western sky, a sliver of red flashing between blankets of black. I keep my eyes on the brightness and imagine holding on to that red rim, flying with it beyond the sunset to where dawn breaks over the sleeping lands of night, as if by traveling with the sun I can cheat the coming darkness.

Turning back, I watch Barney move about in a patch of grass, his fur and flesh, those sweet brown eyes, and that sturdy body that thumps with a musical resonance when given a good pat. I want to breathe him in, fill myself to the core with all he is and all he has been so when the time comes that my hand reaches out to touch him and he is not there, I'll still have something to hold on to.

CHAPTER 36

SPRING 2006

A HAWK GLIDES THROUGH THE CLOUDY APRIL SKY, FLYING JUST above the tree cover of the Twisty Tree Trail where it intermittently appears and disappears, wings fully spread to catch the currents on the breeze. At one point, the trees part to reveal a gray slice of sky into which the dark silhouette once again glides into view. The bird kites downward on the wind, dipping low enough for me to identify the pale chest, dark head, and orange-rust feathers of a red-tailed hawk. He circles above us, scanning the woods. I wonder who his victim is. A vole? An injured bunny? Baby squirrels?

We follow the sharp curve on the trail. The hawk banks to the right with us and sinks lower, hovering above the tree canopy. He disappears for a moment, then returns, gliding high over our heads. It appears he's following us. Recalling the Chihuahua who was snatched from its yard near here, I think of how my lame dog must look to this hawk. Tilting my head to the sky, I yell, "Go away. You're not taking my dog." The hawk flies off but glides right back. I pull the corners of my coat away from my body so I look big, bigger than I am, and flap it back and forth like giant bat wings and stomp my feet as I look up and scream, "Don't count on this dog, you'll be waiting a long time."

I mean it. Barney is a survivor, stronger than I could have ever imagined. On that warm day in February, when we walked the Orchard Trail, I was sure he wouldn't make it to the end of the month. But he has, making it though March to April, celebrating his fifteenth birthday—one hundred and five in dog years—making him a virtual Methuselah of a mutt. Each day, some new humiliation befalls him—the blue plaid doggie diaper he has to wear at home because of the loss of bladder control, tumbling off the backseat onto the car floor when I brake for sudden stops, falling when he stops to lift his leg to pee. Yet every time something awful happens, Barney bounces back in spirit, if not completely in body. He still loves tummy scratches and slappy head sessions and twice-a-day meals of microwaved hamburger and rice. He is grayer, slower, less steady, less able to control his functions, but still obviously in love with life.

By May, the park fills with the scent of honeysuckles and wild roses, but it's so difficult getting Barney in the car that I find myself taking him there less and less. One warm, spring morning, I leave him at his post in front of the dining room window and drive to the library, passing the park on the way. It's in the eighties and so summer-like that on the way back I roll the windows down and turn into the park at the very last minute.

The sun feels good on my skin as I walk across the meadow. Several yards away, a man throws a ball to his Golden Retriever. The dog is loose, which is illegal in this park, but since Barney's not with me, I don't say anything. I'm surprised at how thick and green the trees are since my last visit. Cornflowers and marigolds dot the grass. It's as if winter was all a dream.

With the meadow behind me, I cross the road and head over to the access path leading to the Shark Trail. At the section where the trail begins, I hesitate. To my right is the wooded part of the trail, to my left, the more open area of the wetlands. I step out and walk a few yards down when it hits me that I'm all alone. *No Barney. No husband. Nobody with me at all.* If I walk any farther, there will be no going back, no easy exit out of here. My eyes fall on the wetlands up ahead and the narrowing path. I can feel my shoulders slumping, my back rounding in retreat. Walking out in the open fields and on the roads of the park is not a big deal anymore. But not the trails. Turning around, I walk back to the park road and follow it past the meadow to my car.

Within a few weeks, Barney's bladder problem worsens along with his ability to control his bowels. There are times when he messes himself in awful ways, falling in his own waste, unable to get up by himself. Throughout it all, I try to stay cheerful, pulling him up, dragging him outside, breathing in the overwhelming odor of urine before hosing him down and scrubbing him with baby shampoo. Taking care of him has become a full-time job. I am no longer simply a woman with a dog—I am a nurse and caretaker, as fully invested and involved in my companion's well-being as any individual caring for a seriously ill loved one.

This is what owners of very old dogs do not talk about, not even to other dog people. Caretakers of the infirm elderly have support groups, hospice, expert advice, but I have nothing—worse than nothing, the ever-present threat of judgment. *He's only a dog, isn't he?* So I don't reveal the endless tasks I undertake on his behalf or the fear and despair I feel as I watch my beloved friend slip away.

I pass by the park every time I go to the drugstore, a trip I make frequently for diaper pads or creams to soothe the rash on Barney's irritated skin. But on a warm day in late June, I take Barney to the park for a walk. He does well during our short trek down the Shark Trail, but on the way back to the car his legs go rubbery, and he falls onto the grass just as we reach the road. I'm used to him falling by now, but this time, it's different. His eyes are open and he's breathing okay, but his body is immobile. He just lies there, doesn't even try to sit up.

A car slows down. The driver asks, "Is your dog okay?" I say yes, though it's a lie. The car drives on. I wait at Barney's side until his breathing returns to normal. When I'm able get him upright, I discover he's unable to stand on his own and has peed all over himself. I drag him to the car, my arms wet with piss, which I rinse off with bottled water. And then, instead of taking him home, I drive to the liquor store to buy a bottle of wine—two bottles, because I need to not feel any of this.

The days blur, become a week, no more. We go to the park only one more time and make it a short walk, so that what happened before will not happen again. At night, I sit with his head in my lap and tell him I love him and it's okay for him to leave, but he will not leave, this dog that loves life so much.

The first Sunday in July, my husband and I spend the good part of the day on our boat. When we come home, Barney is in the same place I left him, lying on his side with some of the pieces of the Scooby snack I gave him scattered on the carpet next to him. Instead of getting up, he lifts his head in greeting, then lays it back down, taking my heart down with it. He rises when dinner is called, but eats from a seated position, something he's never done before. When he hobbles away from his bowl, his right leg knuckles under in the exact same manner as the left. It's obvious now why he's had so much trouble standing. The neurological damage has spread.

Two years ago in the park, I made a promise to both of us. I said as long as he could walk, I would do anything I could to keep him alive. But he cannot walk anymore—not with both back legs out of commission. He can barely stand up.

That night, I sit next to him on the carpet, stroking him, talking to him, wishing, hoping he would do this thing on his own, leave in the night and not make me do what I have decided I am going to have to do. But in the morning, when I come downstairs, he is still waiting for me, lying in the same place I left him, tail thumping on the floor as I walk into the room.

I'd like to say I took it well. That all the work, all the grieving, all the preparation and reading and meditation helped me take his final walk with him gracefully and in peace. But I'd be lying. C.S. Lewis said, "No one ever told me that grief felt so like fear." Fear and a special kind of madness.

On the way to the vet, I stop at the park, determined to take Barney for one last visit. But we're in my husband's car and there is no park sticker on the vehicle. The woman at the gatehouse refuses to let us in unless I pay the $5.00 fee.

I plead for her to let us in, tell her that my dog is sick, that he is dying, and I have a sticker just not on this car, please, please let us in. She refuses. Curt waves a five dollar bill in front of my face. But I will not pay because I am insane by now. How can she do this to us? This is our park, it's not right, none of this is. I turn around and stop at the side of the park road near the exit, rolling down Barney's window so he can smell the fragrance of his beloved park. Then we go. Anger has overtaken my grief. It clears my head enough to get me across town to the doctor's office.

At the vet, they lay a beach towel on the floor for him, blue with spinning basketballs on it, a good blanket for a boy dog. I sit next to him and stroke his head. The doctor gives him a tranquilizer and leaves the room so I can sit with him alone for awhile. Then he comes back in and I nod. The needle slips through Barney's skin. And in the time it takes to exhale, he slips away easily, peacefully, as if he's been holding his breath a very long time.

When I walk out of the vet's office with a clipping of his short black fur in my hand, I'm in a state of shock. It's still sunny out, the pines as green as ever, the sky as blue as when I walked in. But it's a different world. Barney is not in it.

CHAPTER 37

SUMMER 2006

FOR MONTHS, I STAY AWAY FROM THE PARK, ALTHOUGH IT'S IMPOSsible to avoid it completely. Every time I go to the library or the bank or the drugstore, I pass by the entrance with its plantings of Russian sage and butterfly bush, the white gazebo with the fancy fretting, the pale green cement pond shooting up its flume of water. It's a constant reminder of my loss. I can't stand to look. But I can't look away, either.

The second Tuesday in August, on my birthday, I stop by the drug store across from the park. When I leave the store, my feet take on a mind of their own, walking past my car, across the street, and around the closed gates of the park into the lush green of a summer's day. With each advancing step, the park unspools before me in all its summer glory: row after row of deciduous trees bending under the weight of their leaves, the smell of tar rising from the road, the woods calling with their promise of cool relief, and everywhere, the vegetal pull of green—in bushes, on trees, on all those unnamable, unknowable plants and vines weaving through the underbrush, green that enters me like a living breath. I want to weep at the sight of it. How could I have stayed away so long?

I pass the pond, the gazebo, and then the low-lying bushes where Barney would always lift a leg. At the directional signs I turn left like I did with Barney, then I take another left at the doggie bag dispenser, passing the houses bordering the park and the yard with the sheltie that always used to bark at us. When I come to the exercise station with the low push-up bench, I pause, exactly like I used to with Barney. The trail narrows at this point, passing through an isolated expanse of woods and wetlands barely wide enough to keep a safe distance from passing dogs. But today it's people, not dogs, I'm thinking about.

For the first time in over thirty years I am walking into the woods alone, without a friend or husband or four-footed guardian. The section of trail before me winds through a shaded area so cut off from the rest of the park that for an eye-blinking moment it resembles the dark hole of hell. I stand at the threshold, envisioning the bend up ahead, and imagine a man lunging toward me. A quickening breath flutters in my chest. For a fleeting moment, I consider turning back. But before I know it, I'm moving into the shade of the trees, acting on an innate sense that it's safe to continue. The cool beauty of the woods sinks into my bones.

Beyond the trees, the wetlands emerge, very dry from weeks of drought. A butterfly dances between exhausted stalks of sea oats, searching for some small bit of moisture. Since Barney's death, the butterflies have been every-where, dazzling in their numbers and variety: Monarchs with startling orange plumage, yellow and blue Swallowtails, tiny cornflower-blue Cabbage Moths, even rare black and white Zebra Swallowtails. Why, in a season of loss, have I been seeing so many butterflies?

A few feet down the trail, the answer comes easily, as if floating down on a powdery wing. Butterflies symbolize transformation—the death of one form and the birth of another. At this time of grieving, it's comforting to be reminded there are possibilities beyond my comprehension.

Past the wetlands, an ancient cedar Barney always liked to stop at tow-ers above the trail. My hands instinctively reach for the shaggy bark. "You outlasted my old boy," I say, patting the trunk. The ragged texture of the bark feels good against my skin. I move closer and closer still, my body collapsing against the tree as my arms embrace the comfort of its closeness, the absolute *there-ness* of its weight and matter. I breathe in its rootedness and the faint piney scent of endurance until I feel rooted myself. Then I let go and continue down the trail. The lack of fear in my body, the hyper-vigilance that always was present when walking alone, fascinates me. It's simply gone. I might as well be walking with Barney.

After several yards of tree-covered shade, the trail opens to the sky. The sun beating down on the asphalt path is relentless. Sweat trickles down my arms. I hear a dog panting behind me and turn around, half-expecting to see a long pink tongue flopping over crooked teeth, but there is no "Tonguey" behind me, no "Panty Boy," no "hot-buttered Barn," only a yellow Lab huffing beside his owner. I smile and nod and let them pass, and as they do, the panting becomes louder. After they're gone, I break down right there in the middle of the trail, undone by that beautiful, slobbery sound.

On the way back, I stop every few feet as if Barney is there with me, sniffing a bush, peeing on a tree, checking out a scent on the trail. Each small pause is just enough to see, hear, smell, touch, and taste the magic of the moment. There's a hint of coolness on the breeze. A voice in the wind whispers *Something's coming,* and something is, I can feel and smell it—a storm, a front, a change of direction. The leaves nod and bend as I walk past as if saying, *Hello, welcome back.* Overhead, two crows dart across the sun-scorched sky giving me the once-over with their beady eyes cawing, *Get on with it, move on.* And I am moving on, pushed along by the great wave of life itself, as real as the chorus of cicadas pulsating in the background, rising and falling in pitch like the swelling tides of an invisible sea.

I feel many things out here: wonder, joy, a sense of aliveness I haven't felt since losing Barney. But what stands out the most is what *isn't* here: the obsessive thoughts, the electrifying fear that used to pulse through my body when walking alone. In its place is solidness and lightness—the weight of my feet on the ground, the ease of breath entering and leaving—the ability to be comfortable in my skin and confident enough to let the world enter it fully. With each step, I can feel how I have changed on a cellular level. I am completely different from the woman who first entered this park with Barney.

In the meadow where we first walked is a tree with a heart-shaped scar carved into its trunk, the damage left by a bolt of lightning. I carry that same scar, loss like a carved-out hole in the very center of my being. But above the scarred trunk is new, green life. The tree continues to grow, and I need to do the same. There will be new challenges before me and, inevitably, a new dog; I am one of those people who need the companionship of an animal to be complete. But I no longer need a dog in order to walk among the wild and beautiful.

This morning, I woke up and asked, "Barney, where are you?" Perhaps he's in the wind, in a Labrador's breath, in the soft glow of afternoon light washing over the trees. Wherever he is, he's still walking with me, maybe just out of sight up ahead, pulling me forward—always forward—unreeling that leash longer and longer as we forge ahead into the unknown.

As I pass the marsh grasses, two butterflies swirl by, dipping and gliding before landing on a pile of leaves near my feet. I pause and thank Barney, this park, and whatever it is in the human soul that pushes us to move out of our broken places toward wholeness. Then I step forward and walk into the rest of my life.

ACKNOWLEDGMENTS

Writing this book has been a long and circuitous journey. I spent endless hours wandering down the roads of memory, struggling to find the voice and structure to the story I had to tell. And while I had to find that path on my own, the assistance and support of those who helped me along the way were invaluable in helping me to shepherd this project to completion.

This book would not have happened without the support and assistance of my writing partner, Diana Sperrazza, who provided not only invaluable insight and inspiration but also pushed me to keep going during the toughest times. I am also grateful to Ceil Malek for her thoughtful and thorough feedback on the first draft of this book and to Debra Landwehr Engle for her valuable insight on ways to make the work stronger. Much thanks to Lisa Knopp for both her careful reading of this manuscript and her lessons on the art of braiding (who knew you could pull together so many strands of story?).

It's difficult to find the words to express my thanks to Julie Bondanza, midwife of my voice and my writer self. You have helped me find my way out of the woods and into my life, and for that, you have my deepest gratitude.

Learning how to move through the seasons with grace and acceptance has been one of the most important gifts in my life. I am grateful to Alesia

Willow Montana showing me how to reach beyond the obvious to find magic and meaning in the cycles of life. And special thanks to Karen Rugg for steadfastly accompanying me on this journey.

I also want to thank Cat Pleska and Jeanette Eberhardy for their early encouragement of this work, which propelled me to move forward with it. And thanks to E. Ethelbert Miller for helping me see how to shape a story from a chapter of this book. Also, to my sister, Roberta Vanderslice, for her insight into canine behavior and for being the best first dog I ever had.

I am most grateful to Martha Bates, whose belief in this project gave it a home in the world. Thank you, Martha. It was my great fortune to find you.

Finally, my deepest love and gratitude to Curt Gary, whose love has sustained me and whose talent as a reader and editor surprised me. And to Barney, who lives on in my heart and in these pages.